MEDICINE BALLS

Dr Rob Buckman is probably best known as co-presenter (with Miriam Stoppard) of the long-running TV medical programme *Where There's Life*. Together with fellow medic Chris Beetles, he also wrote and appeared in the comedy series *The Pink Medicine Show*.

He has performed regularly on radio over the years, most recently in his one-man show, *How To Get The Most Out Of Your Body*. He writes a weekly column in *Punch* and is the author of two earlier books, *Out of Practice* and *Jogging from Memory*.

Despite all this, Rob Buckman is still allowed to practise medicine – but only as a doctor. Next of kin have been informed.

MEDICINE BALLS

Dr Rob Buckman

Cartoons by Edward McLachlan

A GRAHAM TARRANT BOOK

DAVID & CHARLES

Newton Abbot London North Pomfret (Vt)

**To Jo and Susan,
and Orville the fruit-bat**

The author would like to express his thanks to *Punch* Magazine for their permission to reprint material which previously appeared in its pages

British Library Cataloguing in Publication Data

Buckman, Rob
Medicine balls.—(A Graham Tarrant book)
1. Medicine—Anecdotes, facetiae, satire, etc.
I. Title
610'.207 R705

ISBN 0-7153-8752-9

Typeset by Typesetters (Birmingham) Ltd, Smethwick, West Midlands
and printed in Great Britain
by A. Wheaton & Co Ltd, Hennock Road, Exeter
for David & Charles (Publishers) Limited
Brunel House Newton Abbot Devon

Published in the United States of America
by David & Charles Inc
North Pomfret Vermont 05053 USA

About this book

The miraculous human body is almost unique in that it is one of the very few things that we all possess that doesn't come with an instruction booklet or any form of warranty. It is with that in mind that I have decided to write this simple volume in the hope that it will enhance our understanding of our bodies, promote the harmony of well-being and encourage a positive attitude to health-care. And maybe make some money.

To bring together the vast number of facts and up-to-date research findings has been a mammoth undertaking, let me tell you, in the course of which I have consulted ever so many learned and erudite sources, including the world's most prestigious scientific, biological and medical journals, eg Claire Rayner. And *The Observer* a couple of times too.

During the creation of this detailed survey of human biology – a labour of love for me really even if I hadn't got to pay for the car with it – all the facts and data have been meticulously gathered then checked and cross-checked with the obsession for detail that has, I believe, become the hallmark of no cross that out Sue and make it the symbol no flagship no that's even worse alright the hallmark of something yes hallmark of me. Or whatever. If, however, one or two errors of omission or commission have crept under my eagle eyes then what shall we say oh then what the hell.

We live in the 1980s. At the moment. And this is the Age of Information when we all – as human beings, as patients and as ratepayers – may legitimately demand more

Information. And Age. And it is in the spirit of this new-found sharing and caring that I offer my humble (in a way) works to an enlightened, informed and paying public.

Good health to you all. And me. Thank you.

Dr Robert Buckmna

Nervesology

Where better to start our voyage of discovery around the human body than at the head? Nowhere, of course, because the head is really like the nerve centre of the body which is scarcely surprising because it *is* the nerve centre of the body. And inside the head is the brain where all your thinking, calculating, planning and predicting is carried out if you haven't got an accountant.

There isn't room here to deal with all the important features of the head, so I've chosen to survey the latest facts to do with the brain and the eye. After all, it's the eye that does all the seeing for the brain, and the brain which tells us what we think of what we saw. Until we get a chance to read the Sunday papers. (*Note: this chapter was written in black and white.*)

THE BRAIN

Biologically speaking, the human brain is the most complex, intricate and organised organ in the whole of the human skull. From as early as the sixth century BC anatomists noted that the brain is characteristically greyish in colour, soft in consistency and crinkled like the backside of an 82-year-old who's been left in a sauna. The main part of the brain is the cerebrum, named from the Latin 'ceres' meaning 'of the old lady' and '-brum', the vernacular diminutive, meaning 'bum'.

The cerebrum consists of two halves, called the cerebral hemispheres. In most people the left hemisphere controls the right side of the body, the power of speech, the ability to draw, play music, smile, think nice things and work for charity. The right cerebral hemisphere, by contrast, contains the centres responsible for scheming, shoplifting, cash deals, adultery and butter subsidies. In Arizona a neurophysiologist found guilty of a bank robbery recently was able to demonstrate that it was the fault of his right cerebral hemisphere which was given seven years, while he was let off with a caution and a commendation for giving useful evidence.

Perhaps the most extraordinary thing about the brain is that so much of it consists of supporting structures or 'glial' tissue as it is called (rhymes with 'vile' but has a silent 'g' as in 'Tate & Glial'). It has been clearly shown that at any one time the amount of brain tissue actually involved in thinking is 0.002 per cent of the brain's cells (falling to 0.00003 per cent in brain death and in commissionaires outside cinemas). Precisely what the rest of the brain is doing all the time is a matter of scientific speculation, though one theory is that it has 'decided' during the first year of life to take early retirement on favourable terms.

THE DOCTOR ANSWERS YOUR QUESTIONS

Q: A close friend of mine, well actually it was me, went to an 'alternative' medicine clinic which recommended that he have a coffee enema. I haven't heard of coffee enemas before – do they have any damaging side-effects?

A: Yes. They ruin the taste of the coffee.

THE FRONTAL LOBES

At the front of each cerebral hemisphere is an area called the frontal lobe, and the frontal lobes control the person's mood in an inhibitory way. Thus they restrain emotion and exuberance, cause depression of the mood, restrict volubility and make you miserable, and are the cerebral equivalent of the Shore Patrol. We know all this because in the 1880s an American called Phineas Gage had an accident with a tamping iron and blew out the front of his brain (during the course of routine enquiries, according to the police). He survived the accident but his personality was changed. He smiled and laughed a lot, swore greatly, stopped going to Bible class, left his wife and eventually became so extrovert and hilarious that the Federal police were forced to make him a Senator.

The euphoric effects of losing the frontal lobes led to the fashionable operation of 'pre-frontal leukotomy', in which a major part of the frontal lobes is removed to cure depression, and it is believed that this accounts for the fact that so many US Senators are patently lacking in brains. Although the operation has now fallen into disrepute (as has the US Senate) we still acknowledge the inhibitory effect of the frontal lobes on expressive, sexual and emotional behaviour when we speak of 'frontal nudity'. Particularly if you're in the expensive seats.

THE MOTOR CORTEX

Not many people realise this, but actually every part of the body is controlled by a specifically designated part of the brain, except in the case of a certain Cabinet minister whose body is believed to be controlled by a seven-foot green lizard called Derek. For the rest of us, however, our movements – which are correctly known as our 'motor functions' in the complex scientific jargon of the RAC – are under the control of the motor cortex. I'm not quite sure what a cortex actually is but when you die there's this thing called a funeral cortex so it must be something pretty expensive. Anyway, each part of the body is represented by a bit of brain and the size of the bit of brain reflects the importance of that bit of the body. Thus in, say, a pianist, the area of brain used for control of the fingers would be very large; in footballers a lot of brain would be used for control of the feet and genitals; in news-readers a lot of the brain is set aside for the eyebrows, and in Italian riot-police most of the motor cortex is assigned to the truncheon.

THE DOCTOR ANSWERS YOUR QUESTIONS

Q: After our recent holiday in Spain, I came home from work early to find my husband dancing with castanets and wearing a red frilly dress – is it anything to worry about?

A: The castanets are two oval-shaped objects which can be seen clearly on the Spanish female (and, in some parts, on the male as well). They usually separate painlessly from the body late in the evening and should normally cause no problem. Out-of-place or 'ectopic' castanets can be a major source of anxiety and embarrassment and I think this is something you and your husband should discuss with your Arthur Murray counsellor.

The Cerebellum It always seems as if you can drink using your left hand and yet have difficulty controlling your left leg

THE CEREBELLUM

The cerebellum is the 'little brain' (literally either 'little old lady's bottom' or 'old lady's little bottom') and is situated at the back of the head below a membrane called the 'tentorium cerebri' and above the collar. The cerebellum co-ordinates voluntary movements, eg walking, jogging, voting etc. When the cerebellum is working correctly it will prevent jerky, exaggerated, uncertain and drunken actions of the body, though in most marriages that seems to be the wife's job.

What is really interesting about the cerebellum is that it's actually the wrong way round. Thus, whereas your right hand is under the control of the left half of the cerebrum, it is co-ordinated by the right half of the cerebellum. That is why it always seems as if you can drink using your left hand and yet only have difficulty controlling your left leg. If you find that the *right* leg is actually creating a problem then it is worth checking that it's yours.

In the Victorian era it was believed that the cerebellum controlled sexual licentiousness and that stimulation of the cerebellum by tight hair-buns caused lust, adultery and promiscuity. Nowadays we realise that those kinds of problems are actually caused by Labour-controlled councils, and that tight hair-buns cause only migraine and vegetarianism.

THE RETINA

The whole business of seeing things depends on a special lining of light-sensitive purple stuff at the back of the eye. This is called the retina, which is the same name given to a kind of foul Greek wine which tastes like Jeypine. This may explain why so many Greek would-be ophthalmologists became alcoholics instead. Anyway, the retina is coloured this rich purple colour that goes white when light falls on it. (I think my cushion-covers must be made of the same stuff.) However, as the retina goes white it releases an electric signal (unlike my cushion-covers) and this tells the brain that the eye is looking at something, ie light (as if it could be looking at anything else!).

I'm afraid I've never been able to understand the next bit, but the idea is that although you might think the eye is like a camera, it isn't. Thus, although there is a sort of picture on the back of the eye, the brain can't see it. And neither, of course, can the eye (because it's looking the other way, I suppose). So the 'picture' just sort of exists as a complicated bunch of electricity (this is beginning to sound like an ICA catalogue), which means that none of us actually ever 'see' anything at all; it's all just electrical static making us think we're seeing the world out there. Which is also true of *Dynasty*.

THE LENS

Now, in order to enable light to fall on to the retina (the eye-stuff, not the wine), the front part of the eye must allow light through it. This means that the lens in the front of the eye must be transparent and that the eyelid must be in the 'up' position. The lens itself has evolved as the most extraordinary piece of natural engineering and has been able to focus automatically on any object at any distance thousands of years before the Japanese cameras could. However, the lens of the eye can go wrong in several ways – thus you can have myopia ('short-sight'), presbyopia ('long-sight', particularly in Scottish priests), uberopia ('oversight'), utopia (loss of colour vision, seeing things in black and white) and hypermetropia (which may be a shopping centre near Leeds).

All kinds of clever technological advances have helped correct lens defects ever since the development of spectacles, which were invented by Henry VIII. Or maybe Benjamin Franklin. In the early fifties there was the invention of contact lenses that can simultaneously correct squint, short-sight and astygmatism. I understand it's called the Playtex living lens ('. . . it lifts and separates'). Scientists in La Jolla are now working on a whole new health philosophy to help America's health-freaks care for their eyesight. They offer courses of eye exercises which are basically a form of visual jogging, contact lenses impregnated with carrot juice, a high-fibre version of Optrex and the ultimate in high-tech ophthalmic health – a Jacuzzi eyebath.

THE IRIS

The iris is the bit of the eye which the pupil is the hole in. It is available in four fashionable colourways – town brown, true blue, Earl Grey and tutti-frutti. The most important fact about the colour of the iris is that it is inherited according to fairly simple laws of genetics, which means that all brown-eyed fathers of blue-eyed children who have less than three blue-eyed grandparents can almost certainly sue someone. Except in Italy, where they can shoot someone.

The iris has recently come into some quite unexpected fame since the invention of a type of alternative medicine called iridology. Followers of this discipline believe that all the illnesses of the whole body can be diagnosed by looking at the iris. As a method of diagnosis, this offers the practitioner a considerable advantage in that his patients don't have to undress – which speeds up the clinics a fair bit. Although conventionally trained physicians would argue that it takes away part of the fun. I'm sorry, I mean clinical challenge. Anyway, iridologists have constructed charts of the iris showing where the bits of the body are represented like figures round a clock. As a matter of interest, the gall-bladder appears at four o'clock, the colon is at six o'clock (which is just right for when you get back from the office) and the genitals are at eleven o'clock just before close-down.

There is, of course, a major snag in iridology – that is, how can you interpret diseases around the body when the iris itself gets inflamed, as in the condition called iritis? Does this mean that all the other parts of the body should get inflamed in sympathy like a sort of visceral General Strike? I asked several iridologists what they would do if they tried to diagnose a patient who had iritis – half of them said they would read the tea-leaves instead, and the other half said they would call their GP.

THE SCLERAE

The sclerae is (or are) the white bit of the eye around the iris. I think they are named after a group of vengeful Norse goddesses who hung around battlefields waiting to suck the blood of freshly-killed heroes and claim on the insurance. This explains why the day after a major exertion on a modern-day battlefield (eg the office party) the white bits of your eyes go pink. Some animal species including albino rabbits have pink eyes permanently, whereas other species seem to go to the office parties permanently and never get pink eyes at all. So it all goes to show there's no justice in the world after all. The sclerae can also go yellow as happens when you get jaundice. This is a very important sign for us hospital doctors to notice because it may be an early warning of infectious hepatitis and will help the doctor to take early appropriate action, eg not letting the patient out of the ambulance.

Beautyology

As the old saying goes, 'beauty is only skin deep', although actually it would be more accurate to say 'beauty is only skin'. Though not as memorable. The point is that our skin is nature's first bulwark, the interface between our innards and the cold, sharp outside world. But the skin is much more besides. A lot much more besides in fact, as we shall find out in this chapter. Probably.

KERATIN

Keratin is the most important protein component of skin and of all the things that grow in skin, so that it is found all over the animal kingdom, mostly as dandruff. The most extraordinary thing about it is that it can be extremely fibrous (eg bird's feathers), very soft and downy (eg rabbit fur) or terrifically tough and horny (eg Burt Reynolds).

Despite its many wonderful functions most people are only aware of this wonderful protein in its biologically least versatile form, ie the ring round the bath. Even more astonishing is the fact that keratin can also occur as an inflammable liquid which can be burnt to give heat and light, or maybe that's kerosene, but the principle's the same anyway. The NASA space laboratories in America have recently revealed that samples of dust and rock from the moon contain no keratin at all. This means that either there is no life on the moon, or there is life but it doesn't have dandruff.

CELLULITE

Cellulite is an entirely new form of human fat recently discovered by French cosmetic surgeons. It occurs most commonly under the skin of ageing French women, and like most things that live under the skin is very unsightly so that it's just as well that it can't be seen. It flourishes and enlarges in the warmer parts such as the inside of the thighs, the buttocks and the Seychelles.

No one knows for certain whether or not cellulite causes any diseases but French surgeons, at the forefront of preventive medicine, are removing it from French ladies in large quantities just in case. It is not known what happens to all the cellulite that they remove but there was a plan to ship it to Russia in strong steel containers, only Greenpeace found out and stopped it. Enriched cellulite (as the hexafluoride) is the starting material for many lethal substances including heart attacks.

ACNE

This is a very embarrassing skin condition that causes a variety of skin lesions including the comedo (or 'whitehead'), occluded comedo ('blackhead'), adipose comedo ('fathead'), sebaceous macule ('skinhead'), vesicle ('welkie'), or pustule ('honky'). The cause is unknown, but anthropologists in Samoa have discovered a tribe of gorillas in which acne in the male apes seems to serve as a signal to the female apes. They run away. No one knows what this means in sociological terms.

It is thought that acne, by causing pain, embarrassment and moderately deep scars, is nature's way of preparing pubertal males for what it feels like to be married. Skin specialists, who are known as dermatologists in mixed company, have subdivided acne into five categories depending on the type of skin lesion and the salary of the patient. Recent research on the excretion of skin lipids and mucopolysaccharides has suggested that all types of acne, particularly the mild forms, are best treated by a new form of alternative therapy called 'going privately'.

THE DOCTOR ANSWERS YOUR QUESTIONS

Q: I have unwanted facial hair.

A: Thank you, but I have enough of my own.

Acne Acne in the male apes seems to serve as a signal to the female apes

EYEBROWS

Eyebrows are a very common source of dissatisfaction. In evolutionary terms, eyebrows were formed as the facial hair of our ape ancestors retreated from the upper lip during the Ice Age. As it did so it left isolated pockets or tufts up the nostrils and above the eyes before settling into its present position in modern man, ie on the head and hairbrush. This means that in evolutionary terms our eyebrows are the closest reminders we have of our ape-like progenitors, apart from our behaviour at football matches.

Eyebrow transplants enjoyed some popularity in the late 1970s until the famous Guppert and Dietz case where a recipient received one male eyebrow and one female eyebrow which not only met in the middle but had a family and reforested the recipient's entire face. The surgeon concerned was not actually struck off but there's no doubt that eyebrows were raised.

FOLLICLES

Follicles are not at all what you think. They are actually the tiny little sockets in the skin that each individual hair grows in, or, if you are balding, falls out of. I seem to remember that when you are born you've already got all the follicles you're ever going to have and if you lose any, they are never replaced, even if you ask ever so nicely. I believe that you need double-follicles to make a beard and it turns out that Red Indians can't grow beards because they don't have double-follicles, though they've got all the single-follicles they need and a few to spare. Apparently trichologists from Morgantown, Virginia have a theory attributing the massacre of General Custer at Little Big Horn to a simple case of mass moustache-envy.

HAIR

Hair is a specialised product of the skin that grows in patterns determined by evolution, ie all over the place except the eyeballs. But particularly in places like the axillae or armpits, the nostrils and the downbelows, which are all places that are warm and damp, avoiding direct sunlight or an extremely sandy soil.

Interestingly, the only part of a hair that is actually alive and growing is the tiny bit inside the follicle below (see *Follicle* above) and all of the rest of the hair, whether it's glowing, vibrant, gleaming, bouncy or dry and unmanageable like a packet of cheese straws, is stone dead. Microscopists in Princeton have shown that you can tell if a hair is curly or not by cutting it across and examining it under a microscope (round hair grows straight and oval hair grows curly). Other scientists (also from Princeton) have found that you can tell if a person's hair is curly or not by taking their hat off and looking.

NAILS

I wonder if a woman who tears a fingernail while using a shoehorn ever reflects that both fingernail and shoehorn are made of the same material. Well if she did, she would be wrong, because nails are made of keratin (see *Keratin* above), a biologically toughened complex protein fibre, and shoehorns are made of plastic. But rhinohorns, now that's a different matter. Rhinohorns *are* made of keratin and by golly don't we know it, particularly if you try and put your shoes on with one. Even more so if the rhino isn't actually dead.

Incidentally, while we're on the subject of rhinohorns, I'd like to know why it is that keratin in the form of rhinohorn is thought to be sexually attractive and libidinous, whereas keratin in the form of nail clippings in the bath are the exact opposite. Perhaps it's a matter of inter-species signalling, and maybe female rhinos really get turned on by my nail clippings. From what I've seen of female rhinos, they look as though they've got permanent headaches all the time, Saturday or no Saturday. No wonder they're nearly extinct.

Dietology

The idea that 'you are what you eat' is a pretty depressing thought, particularly when you see what goes into hamburgers these days. But actually there's been a lot of interest in diet and vitamins and things just lately, so I thought we'd wipe away the cobwebs of superstition and fantasy and take a long cold sober look at the subject. Then maybe go out for a drink.

VITAMIN C

Vitamin C, as everybody knows, is found in the citrus fruits which are so named because they are beloved of Mediterranean peoples particularly the Citriots. Very high concentrations are found in the orange, the lemon, the pineapple, the ribena, the viola, the guava (or is that a kind of bird excrement? – no that must be guano or maybe gecko). Anyway it was on Shackleton's voyage that the Vitamin C content of limes was discovered, which is why to this very day all English policemen are known as 'Peelers'.

The correct chemical name of the vitamin is 'ascorbic acid' but it got that changed the first week it arrived in Hollywood and has never looked back. It is one of nature's most busy chemicals, acting as a catalyst in promoting biological reactions between two other compounds, like a sort of molecular pimp. As a catalyst, it is needed in many body processes such as when you heal a cut, grow your hair, move your bowels, change your sex or buy shares in British Telecom. If you don't get enough of the stuff, you develop scurvy – a highly unpleasant condition in which your hair falls out, your gums wither, your teeth itch, your skin wrinkles and you look like someone who's spent their life in politics. Vitamin C excess causes ascorbate-poisoning, which causes manic behaviour, staggering gait, vomiting and incontinence. This happens when people drink too much Pimm's.

Eat up your Vitamin C, or you'll never be like your father
Kellogg's
3 Gs
Guava, Gecko & Guano
MP

VITAMIN B12

Vitamin B_{12} compared to the 'Big Sisters' (Vitamins B_1 and B_6) is the Cinderella of the vitamin family, since it was discovered late, was initially thought to be unattractive, and is commonly found in pumpkins and white mice. That said, it's actually a handy little molecule, full of fun and gaiety and deaminated sulphydryl groups. There's a fascinating story about the discovery of the structure of the B_{12} molecule and its two parallel sub-units. It happened in 1921 on an Arctic whaler when the ship's doctor wanted to give the captain an injection of Vitamin B_{12} but didn't have any. So he gave two injections of Vitamin B_6 and that did just as well.

B_{12} was originally discovered as the cure for Pernicious Anaemia – a disease which had a lot of bad press in the 1920s but which is now perceived as a condition that is more misguided than actually pernicious. B_{12} is found in raw liver but then so are quite a lot of unpleasant gritty things that look dark green and may or may not be truffles. More research is required on this point.

VITAMIN E

Vitamin E is surely the most enigmatic character of the whole vitamin society. Nobody knows where it comes from, what it does or how it makes its living. The only fact that is known for certain is that if you deprive male laboratory rats of Vitamin E, they become sterile. However, this is not a particularly reliable method of contraception and female laboratory rats would be advised to take other precautions. You know what I mean, girls.

In Man, and particularly in Wholefood Man, Vitamin E is sold as the elixir of virility, potency, charm, personal magnetism, and fecundity. Mind you, they said all that about Brylcreem and it never got me anywhere. All I can say as a doctor is that if you sprinkle Vitamin E behind your ears you will have no difficulty attracting female laboratory rats.

THE DOCTOR ANSWERS YOUR QUESTIONS

Q: Am I overweight?

A: No, of course you're not. Stop moaning and come to bed.

SILICONE

Silicone is not a vitamin as much as a trace element. It seems to have caused a great deal of fuss lately but I can't remember why. I think I remember being told that silicone in your diet is particularly important if you want your breasts to grow bigger but I can't recall precisely what the silicone does or how it gets there. Perhaps it doesn't actually make them grow but simply gives them the extra polish and shine once they've grown. Anyway, silicone (as in breasts) must not be confused with silicon (as in computer chips). This is difficult because they're actually the same thing. I believe there was a young woman in Utah who had so much silicon in her breast tissue that when she stood next to an X-ray machine they could use her as a word processor.

BROWN FAT

Brown fat is a misnomer (like the Holy Roman Empire which wasn't any of those things). Thus brown fat is not actually brown, nor is it fat, nor holy, nor an empire. It is actually the biological equivalent of an inefficient factory chimney. What happens is that when you eat food it can either be burnt up to make energy or stored as fat (for up to three months in a two-star freezer). Some people are very good at storing up fat and don't 'waste' their food-energy at all, whereas other people will, after a meal, generate a great deal of heat, eg when they see the bill. This heat is generated by the brown fat which is in the form of two strips of stuff under your skin (and clothes of course) alongside your back. So if you have lots of brown fat, you eat, get hot and stay thin and if you have no brown fat you end up with lots of the other kind of (non brown) fat which is apparently coloured a rather pleasant mauve. Anyway, that's the situation at present though it'll probably all be different under a socialist government.

Chestology

Perhaps if there is one thing that we all take for granted, apart from religious broadcasting, it's the apparently simple act of breathing. Yet how close is this simple act to the hub of Life itself. Very is the answer. It is no coincidence that the word 'anemos' in Greek not only means 'breath' or 'wind' but also 'spirit' and 'life' as well as 'mind' and 'cheap restaurant'. Well, let's take a big breath now and get the facts about breathing 'off our chests'!

BREATHING

Breathing is a terrifically important biological activity and recent research work from Chicago has shown that cessation of breathing is one of the commonest causes of death. Respiratory physiologists reviewing breathing mechanisms in the whole of the animal kingdom have subdivided it into two main forms – breathing in and breathing out. Now the whole point of doing either or both of these is to get oxygen into the body, preferably your own. What is perhaps surprising is that not everything in the world actually uses oxygen – many organisms employ *anaerobic* respiration such as occurs in flatworms at the bottom of ponds, bacteria living inside human bowels, some fungi and most literary agents. The rest of us depend on *aerobic* respiration which evolved first in the Pleistocene era though it didn't get as much press coverage then as it does now with Jane Fonda.

Of course, some things in the world don't use either oxygen or anaerobic respiration, but get energy from entirely different sources, eg diesel. In general though, animals use oxygen and give off carbon dioxide whilst plants use carbon dioxide and give off hay-fever. This is called symbiosis and is the nearest Nature ever gets to socialism.

HUMAN BODY – A

The latest findings fro

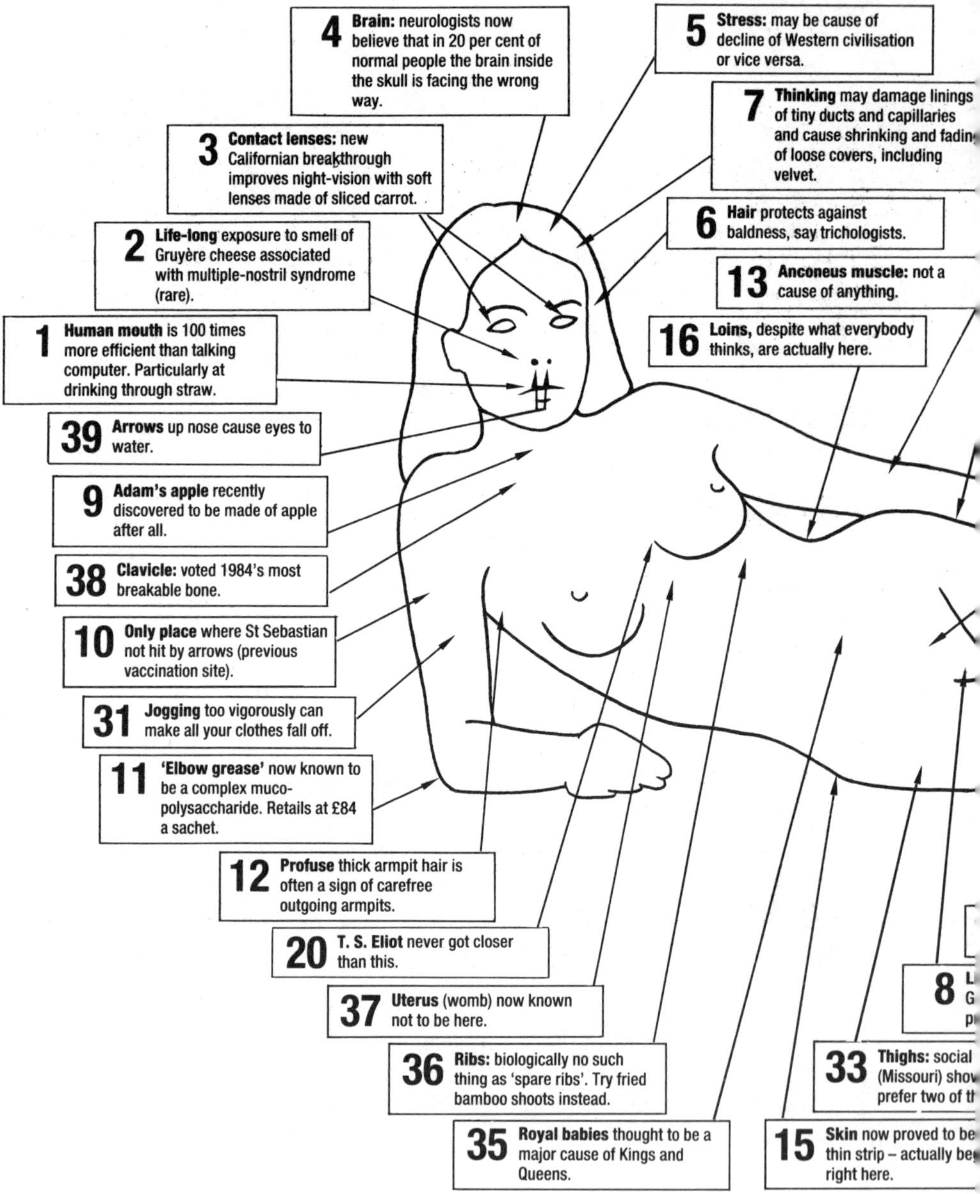

ONISHING NEW FACTS!

ding doctors in America and Britain

eminine itching due to olythene covers over seats of ew Swedish cars (pruritus olvo).

17 **World War III** likely to be caused by minor peri-anal complaints among top politicians, say USA proctologists.

27 **Buttocks** getting smaller year by year. Will be endangered species by 1990.

32 **Cosmetic surgery** can now increase the number of your navels to four (not available UK).

19 **These bits** go flabby early – but often tighten up by next morning.

21 **Calves** now thought to be children of cows. May be cause of veal.

23 **Calluses:** definitely cause bald patches in bath mat.

30 **Air:** not necessary for breathing after all. Sunflower oil can replace.

34 **Breakfast:** now known to be amazing breakthrough cure for night starvation.

24 **Fetishes:** new evidence that fetishes prolong life and lower cholesterol.

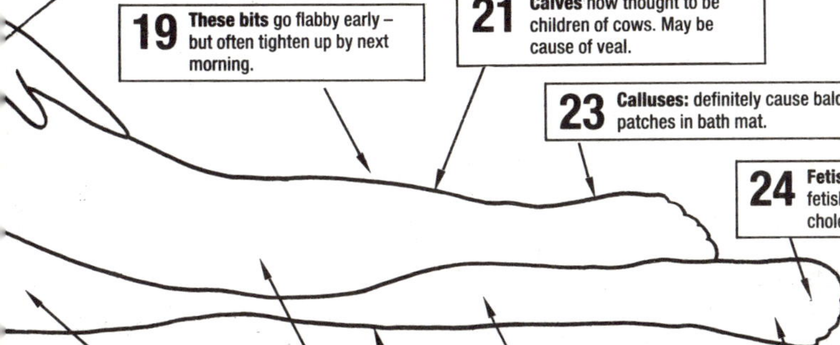

22 **Bust enlargement** should not be attempted if your bust looks like this.

28 **Doctors** can hit you here legally.

26 **Raquel Welch** has chromosomes that reach all the way down here apparently.

29 **Prayer:** might be fattening.

25 **Doctors** think this is ideal height for stocking-tops to ensure maximum visibility and easy handling.

e wash only. No lvents. 5 40

ion and onest cause of sconsin.

THE FIRST BREATH

For years paediatricians have wondered how babies can 'tell' it's time to take their first breath. How do they know they're out of the womb – particularly if that fathead French obstetrician Leboyer has got the lights dimmed to try and fool them they're still inside? How did babies cry before midwives evolved to smack them? How come they've heard of aerobics even if their mothers haven't? How come they can cry first time or do they practise somewhere first? What are little boys made of? What do you call an uncircumcised Jewish baby? (The answer to the last question is 'a girl', but all the other ones are still up for grabs.)

THE LUNGS

The lungs are two huge things that look like pink loofahs. Actually, there are quite a few things inside the body that look like pink loofahs, so if you're a buyer for a transplant surgeon, just be a bit careful before you sign anything. The air gets into the lungs via the nose, mouth, trachea, and main bronchi. Air getting in any other way means you've been stabbed or shot. The function of lungs is to get as much air mixed with as much blood as possible in a small space – like a sort of physiological Royal garden party, only less formal. In order to do this, the lungs' sponge-like structure offers an enormous surface area for gas exchange and it has been calculated that if your lungs were cut open and spread flat over an average tennis court, you'd die.

THE TRACHEA

The trachea is the main airway leading from the mouth cavity down to the lungs. Its name is derived from a big sewer in Rome built by Julius Caesar, or is that the Cloaca or maybe the Via Fallopia? Perhaps the Trachea was Caesar's main airway outside Rome, which I think is now called the Alitalia. Or maybe it was Caligula's horse (hence 'hoarse' as in tracheitis).

The trachea divides into the main bronchi, of which the left one has the sharper turn-off, like the M6 coming off the M1 and with just the same congestion in winter. The bronchi were named after five goddess sisters in Greek mythology who lived on Samos, and spent their lives smoking Capstan full strength and challenging heroes like Odysseus to spitting competitions. The point at which the trachea divides into the bronchi is called the carina which itself was originally named after a Japanese car. This is not to be confused with 'carina' which is Italian for 'dearest one', which is what Caligula called his horse in private and what Caesar called his cloaca (or maybe airline).

THE DIAPHRAGM

The diaphragm is the flat muscular sheet that makes up the floor of the chest cavity and the roof of the abdominal cavity just like in a maisonette. Thus you can think of hiccups as the lungs upstairs banging on the floor when the duodenum downstairs is making too much noise and stopping everyone getting to sleep. The word diaphragm means a thin membrane separating two areas (hence its use in contraceptives) and is derived from the Greek words 'dia' meaning 'no' and 'phragma' meaning 'chance'. When you breathe in, the lungs expand because the diaphragms move downwards, the ribs move upwards and outwards and the bosoms heave. Radiologists in North Dakota, who have spent much time studying respiration in young volunteers, have shown that if a woman has small inefficient diaphragms, widely spaced ribs and large bosoms, nobody minds at all.

THE DOCTOR ANSWERS YOUR QUESTIONS

Q: I'm worried about my legs. Just recently they seem to have developed a greeny brown discoloration which in some places is a bit mottled and flaky.

A: This is obviously verdigris. This condition can seriously mar the appearance of any legs, particularly Queen Anne, although I assume from your letter that yours are more likely to be ball-and-claw. Rub down with ammonia, polish with a proprietary brand of silver polish, buff with a chamois leather and if challenged at Sotheby's, lie about your age.

Some ****
CAPSTAN
FULL STRENGTH
20 CIGARETTES

The Trachea The bronchi were named after five goddess sisters who spent their lives smoking Capstan full strength and challenging heroes like Odysseus to spitting competitions

BRONCHITIS & EMPHYSEMA

These two lung diseases were originally described in 554 BC by Hippocrates, who named them after a firm of Athenian solicitors. Chronic bronchitis (the junior partner of the firm) is a condition of persistent coughing each winter. Some people call it 'smoker's cough' but we doctors tend to think of it in more accurate pathological terms as cougher's cough. Emphysema is a slightly different condition in which the lungs tends to wear a bit thin. If you think of the lungs as being like a string vest, then it's one of life's little mysteries that if you start tearing up a string vest, the more holes you make in it, the fewer holes there are left in the vest. Well, an emphysematous chest is a bit like that, except of course the nipples are on the outside.

THE DOCTOR ANSWERS YOUR QUESTIONS

Q: I've noticed brown spots at the base of my pistils, and yellowing of my stamen.

A: Spray frequently with Bordeaux mixture, re-pot frequently, use less root-food and above all keep away from direct sunlight and stimulating company until it's all over. In case this is infectious, it might be a good idea to burn your towel as well, particularly if it's insured.

THE HEART

The heart is a very interesting organ and is made of specialised muscular tissue that cardiologists call 'heart muscle'. The extraordinary thing about this muscle is that it beats spontaneously without any form of external excitation, stimulation, encouragement, applause or payment for unsocial hours. This was shown in the eighteenth century by William Harvey who took fresh frogs' hearts (unless the Animal Liberation lot were around, in which case he'd use artichoke hearts) and put them in a petri dish of buffered Ringer's lactate, which is a kind of life-supporting broth like a biochemical chicken soup. I seem to remember the heart went on beating until it ran out of glucose (when it became the so-called 'dead Ringer') or maybe until Boris Karloff came in and said, 'The generator's ready, master,' or was that something else?

Anyway, it's jolly lucky that the heart beats without needing humans to remind it, otherwise there'd be a government department in charge of it, and it would be a key target in industrial disputes and we'd all be dead before we knew where we were. Which is sometimes how it feels now.

ECGs

ECG is the acronym for 'Electrocardiogram' which the Americans abbreviate as EKG, which is hardly surprising for a nation that spells day-night as 'da-nite', thinks Benny Hill is funny and takes Ronald Reagan seriously. Anyway, the ECG is the thing resembling ticker-tape from Reuters that doctors in TV series look at by running it through their fingers, and it is a record of the electrical activity of the heart or – to put it into American – a rekerd avthe electrikle aktiveetee avthe hart. It's a bit like those computer diagnostics that garages do for high-performance cars, except with an ECG, if it shows a fault, there's nothing that can be done about it. If it's normal there's no guarantee you're healthy (or even alive) and if it's wrong you don't get your money back. The only thing the ECG can always tell the doctor for certain is whether or not the ECG machine is working, and that surely must count for something in these days of uncertainty and foreign imports.

CORONARY ARTERIES

The heart muscle uses a tremendous amount of energy, mostly in the form of glucose, glycogen, sanatogen, ammonium, euphonium and anthracite. Now, curiously enough, even though the heart is absolutely chock-full of blood and spends its whole day pumping blood all over the place, it doesn't have enough for its own use, let alone any to spare for emergencies. This may sound silly but your bank manager will spin you a very similar yarn. Anyway, the heart gets its own personal blood supply (like dipping its fingers in the till) from three slender arteries called 'coronaries', from the Latin 'corona' meaning a crown. Presumably this usage arose because most Roman crowned emperors died of heart attacks, or that's what it said on the death certificate, though with Italian police even in those days it was probably a matter of falling out of a window during routine inquiries.

Well, the coronary arteries are very thin and easily blocked by stuff called atherosclerosis, which is a porridgy, silt-like substance that's easy to accumulate but difficult to pronounce (the exact opposite of money). In essence, it's a bit like hard water furring up your pipes. By the same analogy, blockage of a coronary artery causing the characteristic pain of angina is nature's way of telling you it's time to phone for the plumbers. The modern technique of transluminal coronary angioplasty is just like Dyno-Rod, and mitral valve disease is just like a sticking ballcock. All of which is why the new plan to privatise the NHS will have GPs and plumbers sharing the same deputising service.

LIPIDS

Now we don't know much about what causes atherosclerosis except that we're pretty damn certain it's something to do with the lipids in the blood. Lipids are a group of chemical compounds very similar to fats except more brightly coloured and slightly cheaper. There are many different kinds of substances in the lipid family including cholesterol, megesterol, virol, clairol and zeppo. Lipids are found in many places on the average English breakfast table – in butter, in milk and in eggs, for example, and maybe there are a few of them lurking behind the salt cellar or hiding in your napkin ring or under your fork ready to nip into the muesli while you're reading the paper.

Actually, I had a friend called Dave who was fanatical about cholesterol and lipids; he wouldn't let an egg-yolk pass his lips (going either way), would not allow cream in the house, could eat *boeuf stroganoff* so skilfully that he'd leave the high-density triglycerides on the side of his plate, and divided his whole life equally between eating salads, bicycling and opening his bowels. He spent so much time and money in a vegetarian restaurant in Oxfordshire that they named the septic tank after him, and yet despite all this he died suddenly at a young age. They found at the post-mortem that his left coronary artery was jammed solid with lettuce leaves.

ANXIETY

Anxiety and stress both affect the heart, causing the release of adrenalin which speeds up the pulse, raises the blood pressure and in turn causes release of fatty acids, thus hastening the process of atherosclerosis. This means that if you are unfortunate enough to have a heart attack and find yourself in an intensive care unit, the one thing you must remember above all other things is DO NOT WORRY ABOUT IT. Because if you do, you'll die.

Nightology

By and large we doctors know there are two major kinds of activity that go on at night: sleeping activity and sex activity, and the one usually precludes the other. Though, of course, there are many things that end up precluding a bit of the other, the commonest being marriage in my opinion. Anyway, seeing as how we spend so much of our time thinking about these two things, isn't it amazing that we know so little about either? Yes it is. Except I happen to know quite a lot about one of them. Only I can't remember which.

Sleep
It's a little known fact that as human beings we spend a great proportion of our waking lives asleep. No, that can't be right, anyway here's an update.

SLEEP

Sleep is a primeval animal motive force like food, warmth and sex, ie nobody gets enough of it. Sleeping is a phenomenon of the higher life forms including mammals, primates, psychiatrists etc, and does not occur among the less evolved vertebrates like jellyfish, toadstools, dentists and so on. Scientists do not know exactly what goes on during sleep – well they wouldn't, would they, because they're asleep during it, same as we are – but some biological measurements have been made, a few of them legally. As a result we know that during sleep the body's basic metabolic rate falls, the respiratory rate decreases, carbon dioxide tension rises, the pound falls on the overnight markets and burglars steal your video.

It has been found that while you're asleep your brain is actually *more* active during sleeping than waking – although those experiments were done on actors, so they may not apply to human beings. What happens is that there is a thing responsible for keeping the brain in 'waking' state. It's called a bank statement. No it isn't, it's called the reticular formation activating system but it has the same effect. Anyway, the 'waking' centre gets switched 'off' when the body receives certain signals, eg somebody else's holiday slides or the start of International Darts. *Now read on.*

THE PHYSIOLOGY OF SLEEP

The electrical activity of the brain can be reduced on a thing called an EEG, and you can do an EEG on someone falling asleep (though you'll need a Home Office permit first so it's easier to tap his phone if you really want to know what's happening). Anyway the first thing you see on the EEG are things called 'alpha rhythms' which are low-frequency, broad-based, high-fibre emissions which have now been banned in Russia. They are a sign that the brain is tucked in and ready to snuggle down. As sleep deepens, the alpha rhythms disappear and various events occur, some of which stop all brain activity altogether (eg breaking wind).

What happens next is really amazing: while the body stays asleep, the *brain wakes up again.* Of course at this point the body can wake as well in response to exceptionally strong stimuli (eg her husband coming home) but usually this is where Rapid Eye Movement (REM) sleep occurs. We know this because we can see the eyeballs rolling around under the lids, and we believe that this is because the brain is awake but can't find the switch to raise the eyelids and is blundering around in the dark. If you wake someone up during REM sleep they may tell you that they were dreaming (see below) at that point, though they are much more likely to tell you to sod off. Which is another reason why sleep is still an enigma.

DREAMING

The activity of dreaming occurs at well-defined points in time, including REM sleep, party political broadcasts, shopping at Tesco etc. However, the exact *significance* of dreaming is still controversial. Sigmund Freud (hah!) believed that dreams are what happens when your Subconscious comes out to play while the Conscious can't bully it or sneer at it. Thus, according to Freud (and you should hear what his mother had to say about him, the big soppy booby), if you dream about factory chimneys it's because of a Subconscious penis-envy (commoner in women) and a dream of male genitals means a

Subconscious chimney-envy, and so on.

Curiously enough, my friend Rod had a recurrent dream in which he found himself making love to Freud's mother. His psychoanalyst (who was a Jungian) said this dream was neither Freudian nor Oedipal but was due to eating cheese blintzes late at night. So Rod stopped eating cheese blintzes and found that the dream changed so that he was making love to Freud's father. So he stopped seeing his psychoanalyst and now dreams about making love to Freud's cheese blintzes. Personally, I don't believe any of this kind of clap-trap. There's a tribe in Polynesia that believes that dreams are caused by the ghosts of dead ancestors entering your brain and monkeying about – this tribe has very many large and well-kept cemeteries and a very few impoverished psychoanalysts, so they may be on to something after all.

SLEEP DISORDERS

There are lots of things that can cause disorders of sleep, the most important of which are young babies. The state of not getting enough sleep is called 'insomnia' and many doctors believe that in most cases this can be cured by being honest with your tax returns. The opposite state is called the 'somnolence syndrome' in which the brain is permanently set in 'sleep' or 'snooze' mode and sufferers from this disease usually do well in nationalised industries.

Other things may upset the sleep cycle, including crossing international time zones – this phenomenon of 'jet lag' causes abnormal sleep, endocrine disturbances including glucose metabolism and menstruation, and slowing of cerebral function (do you remember Henry Kissinger?). Another state which is similar is the hypnotic trance, although we know that this is usually more expensive. Finally, nature's greatest sleep achievement must surely be hibernation in which a huge warm-blooded mammal, eg a bear, can go to sleep for four months without taking a single valium.

THE DOCTOR ANSWERS YOUR QUESTIONS

Q: We have been married for forty years, and my husband still makes love four or five times a week. Is there anything I can do?

A: Try and catch him at it.

Orgasms There is a species of marsupial in which the male has two complete sets of genitals and is thus able to achieve simultaneous orgasm by himself

Sex
It's another little known fact that most of the time that is not spent asleep is involved in some way with sex – usually before, but occasionally afterwards. So it is without apology, fear or favour that in this handbook to the human body, we fearlessly grasp the nettle of sexual arousal. And see why it is that we feel the way we do about sex. If we do, that is.

LOVE AT FIRST SIGHT

Curiously enough there is a genuine biological basis for love at first sight. Schwartz and Eisenmenger, two behavioural psychologists in Florida, investigated the phenomenon in young women using a multifactorial-personality-inventory questionnaire and managed to get several girls back to their place afterwards. And, believe me, Eisenmenger is no oil painting so he must be pretty crafty. Anyway, it seems that instant attraction is not a mystical process or a matter of being destined for each other, it's simply to do with clues we pick up about each other without realising it. For instance, women may subconsciously become aware of subtle attractions that don't reach the level of conscious recognition, eg forcefulness in the neck muscles, a hint of vulnerability in the chin, a glimpse of an American Express card, a sense of humour, confidence, gold, being Prince Andrew etc.

Conversely, men can learn to read 'no go' signals from women, if only they know what to look for. Eisenmenger listed the following warning signs that love at first sight is *not* occurring: turning the shoulder, continuing use of the emery board, saying 'I'll get back to you on this one', vomiting, calling the police or pretending to be dead. Finally, a word of caution: my friend Jeremy met a girl at a party and immediately felt a fluttery-butterfly-whirly feeling in his heart, and it turned out to be a hiatus hernia.

PHEROMONES

Pheromones are fascinating biochemical substances which we exude through our skin involuntarily and which tell other members of our species things about us. Mind you, this definition also applies to sweat, only I suppose sweat isn't a fascinating biochemical substance (unless you're a pervert or a laundry). Other species use pheromones to signal anger or fright or territorial possession, whereas in Man these functions have been taken over by solicitors. Interestingly, biochemists have now identified the woman-attracting male pheromone in humans and have produced it commercially. It's supposed to make a man irresistible to women and to give an aura of macho-butch-virile masculinity. I bought some but I couldn't get the cap off the bottle.

SEXUAL FANTASIES

Many people are worried that their sexual fantasies are abnormal and may adversely affect not only their real sex lives but also their relationships with other people, their social standing and their pension rights. In the last few years since I have become a fully qualified caring and sensitive person, complete strangers have come and told me their sexual fantasies (though they never wait long enough to listen to mine). From that experience, I would say that it is normal to have fantasies about certain public figures, eg Toyah Willcox, Bo Derek, Nancy Reagan, Patrick Moore. On the other hand, I think some sexual fantasies are unhealthy and potentially damaging, eg fantasies about Noddy, electric toasters, earwigs, Joan Collins, pickled onions. Fundamentally, what I believe about living in a fantasy world is: as long as it doesn't cause pain, go ahead and do it. After all, this is 1972.

THE DOCTOR ANSWERS YOUR QUESTIONS

Q: My boyfriend claims that he is a millionaire and that he is Howard Hughes and 108 years old. Is this normal?

A: A lot of people have asked me this question and I have to say that if your boyfriend is Howard Hughes then he is also dead. Rigor mortis may adversely affect your sex life but on the whole I'd think of the money and smile.

ORGASMS

Orgasms have caused trouble for centuries. The exact meaning of the Greek word from which orgasm is derived is controversial. Aristophanes used 'orgasmous' to mean 'earth tremor' or 'cataclysm' whereas his wife used it to mean 'was that it?' A few years ago many women confused orgasms with origami which is a kind of intricate paper-folding and actually much more difficult to fake.

The biological function of the orgasm is not known, but physiologists in New Jersey have shown that different species of animals have orgasms with different frequencies. Orgasms occur least often in rattlesnakes, ants and the virus of German measles, and they occur most often in laughing hyenas and New Yorkers. I'm told that in the Antipodes, there is a species of marsupial in which the male has two complete sets of genitals and is thus able to achieve the much-talked-about simultaneous orgasm by himself – which just about says it all for sex life in Australia.

THE DOCTOR ANSWERS YOUR QUESTIONS

Q: I play rugby regularly and in the showers after a recent match I noticed that I am apparently much smaller than other men. I am now very self-conscious about it. Is there anything I can do to increase my size?

A: Being small need be no disadvantage these days provided there is understanding, goodwill, patience and yes, even a sense of humour, on all sides. Look at Alan Ladd, for example; he was only five foot two (on a good day) and nobody ever said *he* wasn't a lot of fun in the showers. In fact being small can be a terrific advantage, particularly if you're a portable radio-cassette deck. If you're really embarrassed, then get some shoes with elevated heels. You may look a bit silly wearing elevated heels in the showers, but then lots of people look pretty silly in the showers anyway. On the other hand why not take up chess – you spend the whole match sitting down and you won't need to have a shower at all.

THE WONDERFUL WORLD OF MEDICINE

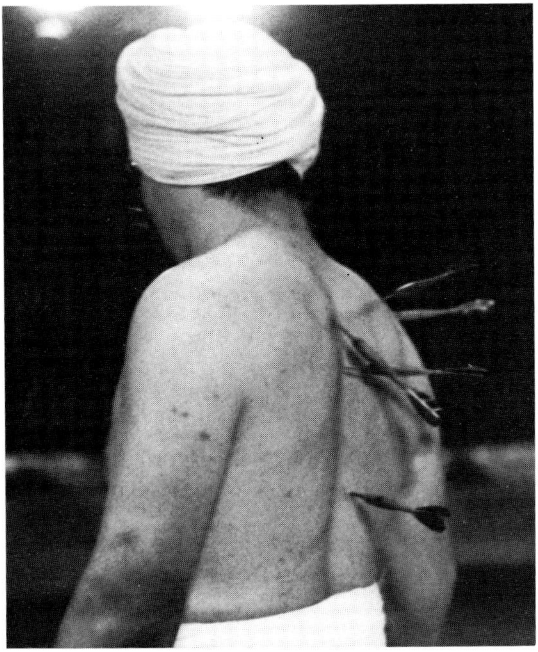

DESPERATE REMEDY

This historic picture shows Mr Ramji Chatterjee, a long-term migraine sufferer, being cured of his symptoms by a new form of long-distance acupuncture. The 'healers' do not hold conventional medical degrees, but claim to have been trained by the Medical Corps of the National Front. The case continues today.

LO-TECH COMES TO OUR HOSPITALS

As the energy crisis begins to bite into the NHS budget, gastroenterologists provide new sources of fuel. Seen here is a sufferer from excessive flatulence who now provides enough energy to light his ward, keep the hot-air balloon up and entertain visiting children with a working model of the Magic Roundabout.

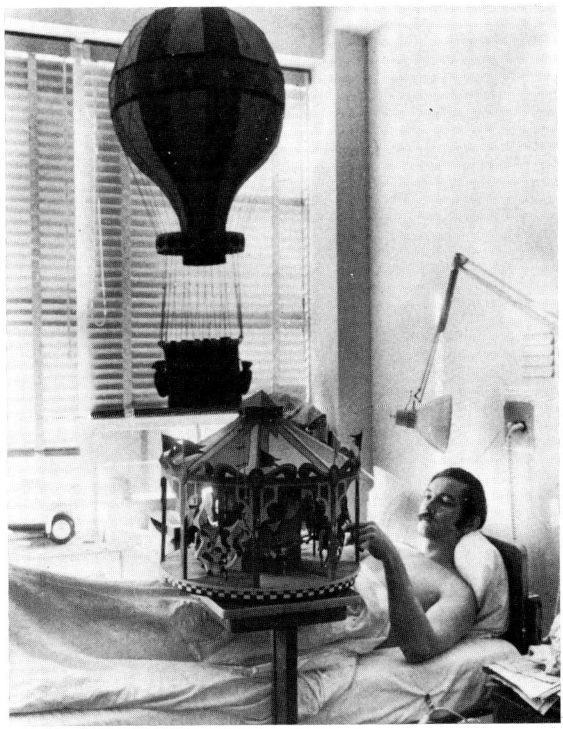

A FIRST FOR BASINGSTOKE!
Visiting dermatologist Toshira Yashica is seen here taking samples for virological analysis from Mr Andrew Hotchkiss, Britain's first case of *rubella dalmatiens* (Dalmatian measles). This rare condition is thought to be caused by accidental contact with Jehovah's Witnesses and affects every part of the body except the socks.

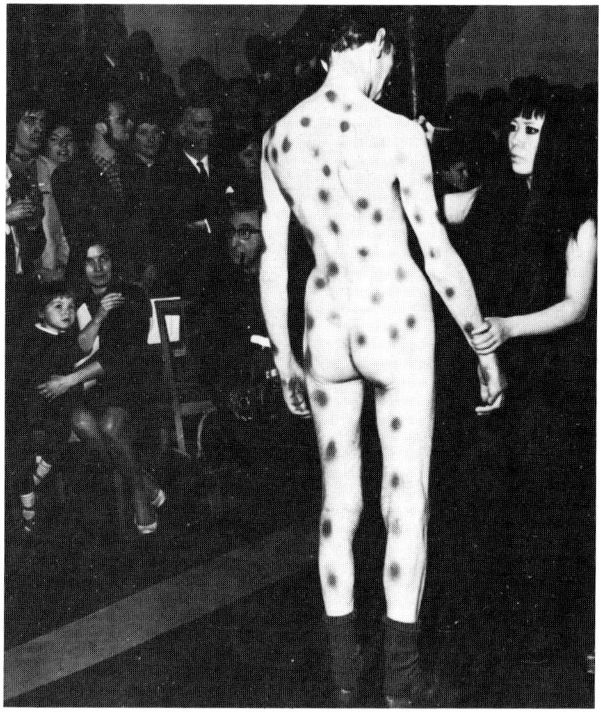

QUO VADIS?
Britain's oldest test-tube baby has been in an incubator for thirty-three years while the local council try to decide whether he should be allowed home with the American couple who have paid his heating bills.

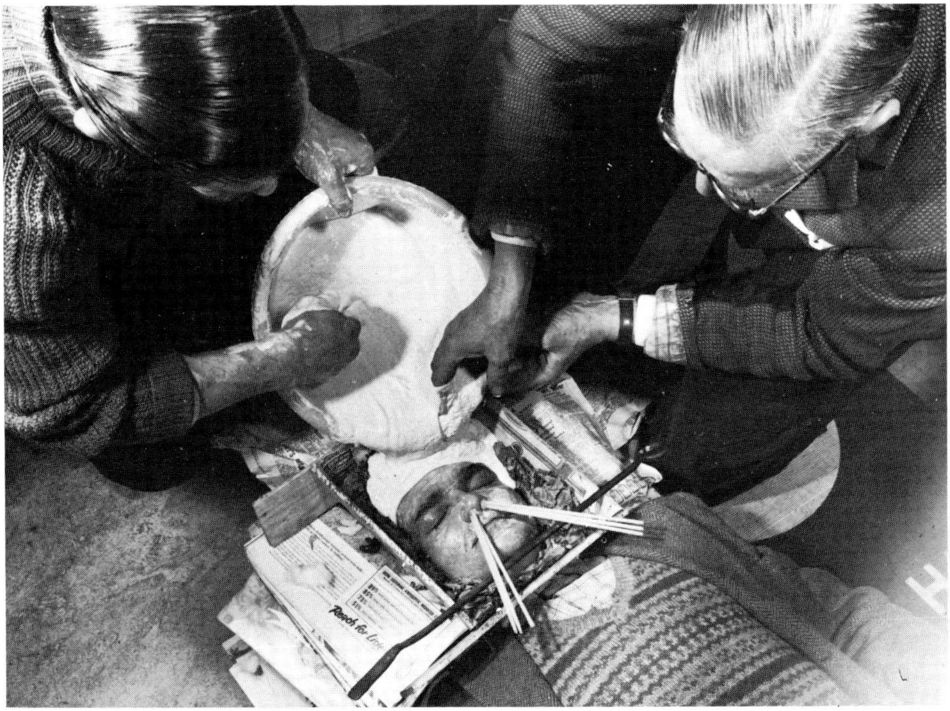

HUNGER STRIKERS BEWARE!
Resourceful medical officers from the Home Office are seen here at Parkhurst Prison dealing with a suspected Italian terrorist's hunger strike by force-feeding him with spaghetti.

SCARSDALE REVISITED
The new North Scarsdale Clinic certainly produces impressive results in crash-course weight-reduction and rejuvenation. Among recent satisfied famous customers are the Everly Brothers (*left and right*).

HI-TECH MEETS HOMEOPATHY

Racing fan and playboy Patrick Double-Barrell (*seen centre after a marvellous party*) was the first client at the Esher Homeopathy Clinic and Racetrack. Doctors Angela Pasteur (*left*) and Thomas Lister (*right*) are seen demonstrating the new homeopathic carbon-monoxide colonic irrigation unit.

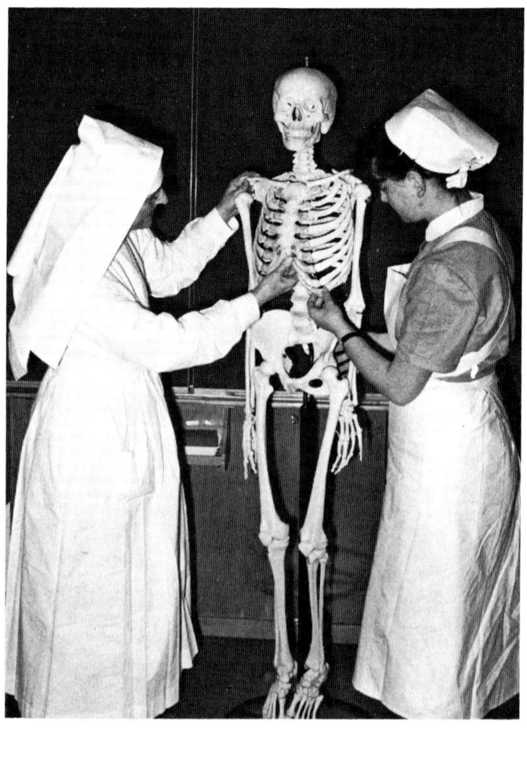

THE TRADITIONAL NURSING SKILLS

In the Vienna nursing school at the resort of Bad Minton, modern nurses are taught the old skills in the fundamentalist way. Here Sister Oberleutenant Schwinkler (*left*) and Nurse Gruppenfuhrer Shriek (*right*) welcome pupil-nurse Anna Endelbaum (*centre*) back from the punishment block.

GUILT ABOUT SEX

When it comes to sex (eventually), there are as many ways of feeling guilty about it as there are of doing it. In fact there are more, since behavioural psychologists in Minneapolis have shown that it is now possible (and legal) to have one kind of sex and feel guilty about it in two ways. Historians believe that guilt about sex began in the garden of Eden after The Fall (apparently about five minutes after) and shortly before The Getting Up Again. Some theologians say that the serpent is the first ever symbol of sexual guilt, whilst others believe it is a prophetic symbol of genital herpes. Still other theologians believe that absolutely everything is a symbol of sex and that sex is just something that one shouldn't do in front of the serpents.

Nowadays, in a more enlightened age, we know that sex causes guilt not because it is fun, but because it is *such* fun, and it's so easy to get caught at it. Modern family counsellors are now able to cure mild sexual guilt by simply fitting a lock on the bedroom door, although this sometimes leads to inter-personal conflicts about who ought to be on which side of it. And with whom. Perhaps the greatest contribution to this field came from the Viennese analyst Ernst Trusthaus-Forte. He showed that early sexual attitudes were reinforced by toilet training which came too early in a child's life, and that sexual guilt could be avoided if they went to the toilet later, say about ten thirty.

Tummyology

Do you ever think about what happens to your food after you swallow it? Well, so do I and a very unpleasant thought it is too. But once the food is out of sight beyond the tonsils, it is in the territory known to us doctors as 'the guts'. I thought that it might be a good idea if we took a look at some of the things that keep on coming up. And also, while we're in the neighbourhood, at a few of the things that surgeons like snipping off or out. (*Note: this chapter has been perforated to become an easy-to-cut-out guide.*)

FLATULENCE

Flatulence is the word we use to describe the passing of collected air from the large bowel into the atmosphere. 'Farting' is the word we use when other people do it. Chemically speaking, the gas itself is largely derived from the enzymatic activity of bacteria living in the colon and can give scientists valuable information about their metabolism. Particularly in a lift or phone-box.

Colonic gas is rich in methane and low-molecular weight sulphides and many other ingredients commonly found in acid rain. These residues represent unconsumed energy and it has been calculated that under controlled conditions the average burst of flatulence could illuminate a large ballroom, or under other circumstances empty it. The formation of large quantities of gas is encouraged in the context of a high-fibre diet, and is discouraged in the context of a public library. Harley Street dieticians have worked out a way of coping with habitual and excessive flatulence. They stare at the person standing next to them and blame it on them.

STOMACH

The stomach is really a biochemical cauldron for mixing food with digestive juices and is named from the Spanish word 'estomach' which means 'disgusting'. The stomach contains very strong hydrochloric acid though no one knows how it manages to smuggle it in without dissolving the teeth. As you probably know, gastric acid is strong enough to burn a hole in a carpet. This was discovered by doctors treating a man called Alexis St Martin whose stomach just happened to be lined with Axminster Floral.

We now know that stomach ulcers are caused by worry and a recent survey of 320 Italians being investigated for ulcers revealed that the commonest cause of their worry was the thought that they might have an ulcer. Behavioural therapists are now working on a positive-thinking approach to the condition in which people are trained to believe so strongly that they haven't got ulcers that the problem disappears. Mind you, they tried that with unemployment and look what happened. Ulcers used to be status symbols. So did Anna Ford.

OESOPHAGUS

The oesophagus is a flexible muscular tube leading from the outside world via the mouth to the stomach or vice versa as in being sick. It conducts food downwards by a movement called 'peristalsis' in which one bit pulsates and then stops and then the next bit pulsates and then stops and so on. This is basically the same mechanism that snakes use when they walk, only slower and noisier.

The oesophagus is divided into three parts or 'thirds' but fortunately they're all joined together. The bottom third (or 'bosphorus') is joined to the stomach and is thus able to participate in many of the exciting functions of gastric mucosa, eg catching ulcers. Birds have very interesting oesophaguses which have a ballooned bit in the middle which is full of stones which grind up their food for them, which is just as well since they haven't got any teeth. In Man the middle third of the oesophagus (or 'sarcophagus') can also become filled with stones, or it certainly feels like that after you've been drinking vodka.

Dammit, ma
can't you kee
in tune wit
the bloody

Flatulence It has been calculated that under controlled conditions the average burst of flatulence could illuminate a large ballroom

DUODENUM

The duodenum is a thin piece of gut named after the 'duodena', an attic or corridor in an emperor's villa usually filled with boxes of winter clothes or odd boots. In the gut, the duodenum leads from the gastric antrum (or 'pantry') to the jejunum (or 'garage') via the ampulla (or 'front-porch') to the mesentery (or 'rose-garden'). The main function of the duodenum is to allow the digested food coming from the stomach to mingle with pancreatic juice and bile in an intimate and informal environment with exciting decor, cheap wine and the ethnic atmosphere.

The duodenum, like the stomach, can develop ulcers but is less inclined to do so, probably because it's generally less tense, takes more holidays and spends most weekends at the cottage. The contents of the duodenum are not acid but alkaline, and far from burning a hole in a carpet can actually be used to remove ink stains from rayon and machine-washable fabrics. Using modern fibre-optics it is now possible to look right down into the duodenum but to be quite frank it's hardly worth it since it's not exactly Sophia Loren's boudoir down there. All things considered, the duodenum is the least attractive part of the gut with the possible exception of the haggis.

PHARYNX

The pharynx is situated right at the back of the mouth and is the bit that we doctors can't quite see when patients say 'ah'. The walls of the pharynx contain over nine hundred separate muscles whose job is to make sure your food doesn't go down into your lungs, though they're not so good at stopping it going up your nose if someone makes you laugh while you're eating trifle.

The back of the pharynx is rather badly designed and food and stuff, eg meat, can often get lodged there, sometimes causing respiratory embarrassment in a situation known in America as 'sudden death'. This can be dealt with quickly using something called the 'Heimlich manoeuvre', I think, or maybe that's the practice they've just outlawed in Utah. Anyway, if the Heimlich manoeuvre is the thing for getting meat out of throats or horse's hooves, and if you're interested in finding out more, please send me a stamped addressed envelope and I'll give you full details and some pieces of meat rescued from sudden death in this way.

TONSILS

Tonsils are so named from the Middle English word 'tonce' or 'taunce', meaning 'a nightmare' or 'something highly unpleasant and squashy' (usually applied to something that is stepped in), and the suffix '-il', meaning 'it sticks in your throat'. They are two blob-shaped organs situated on either side (usually both) in the delicate and sensitive oropharyngeal area to make sure they cause maximum pain when inflamed.

Tonsils are actually made of lymphoid tissue which (in childhood) is immunologically very active – this is just as well since it is certainly not decorative. The tonsils can be considered as the front-line soldiers of the defence system but in most six-year-olds they behave like conscientious objectors. After they have been removed they can be kept in a glass jar but require plenty of light and regular re-potting.

ADENOIDS

The adenoids are very similar to the tonsils only more so. They are situated in that delicate no-man's-land of sinuses behind the cheek bones which isn't quite nose but isn't really eyes or brain either. The word 'adenoid' ends in -oid which means 'a bit like' (as in 'android' – a bit like a man; 'asteroid' – a bit like a star [eg Joan Collins]; 'anthropoid' – a bit like a dead Russian premier). It's difficult to say exactly what it is that the adenoids are a bit like, except the tonsils, in which case they should be called the 'tonsilloids', but they aren't. In pre-Roman Sicily, the adenoids were regarded as exalted organs and bringers of good luck and great fortune, but this all changed in 210 BC when the entire population was wiped out by an epidemic of virulent sinusitis.

APPENDIX

The appendix is an evolutionary hang-over from the days when man was a non-carnivorous peace-loving grazing vegetarian animal – ie the 1960s. It still serves a useful function in the rabbit where it is full of bacteria that digest the grass the rabbit eats and turn it into something else, I forget what – maybe milk, or perhaps that's cows. Anyway, it has been calculated that if man ate vegetables the way a rabbit does, we would require an appendix the size of a golfbag only in a lighter brown. As it is, the appendix is so small and squiggly that it often gets inflamed and needs to be removed. This is done by the operation of appendicectomy, often incorrectly abbreviated to 'appendectomy' by Americans who like to shorten everything especially if it requires hospitalisation. This operation was known in Ancient Egypt but you had to go privately.

HAEMORRHOIDS

Haemorrhoids don't quite fit into the category of bits of you that can be snipped off easily, but it's true to say that once they have been removed, no one has ever asked for them back. They are another thing that ends in -oid and are therefore 'a bit like' whatever 'haemorrh' means – an informal poll conducted among fifteen sufferers concluded that 'haemorrh' means 'sitting in sulphuric acid'. In colloquial parlance they are known as 'piles' (which, by coincidence, is French for batteries – a point to be borne in mind in France when consulting a proctologist or buying a torch). It is not known why they are called 'piles' apart from the fact that Harley Street proctologists are very wealthy and when seen in Rolls-Royces are jocularly referred to as 'pile-drivers'.

THE DOCTOR ANSWERS YOUR QUESTIONS

Q: I have just noticed a little swelling in my left groin and I have been feeling a little off-colour. Could this be the Black Death?

A: Frankly I doubt it. The Black Death was frightfully popular a few centuries ago but now is rather a collector's item. Early symptoms include dizziness, nausea and a ringing in the ears caused by people outside with bells asking you to bring out your dead. Lots of things cause swelling near the groins and the commonest cause is carrying too much loose change, but if I'm wrong and you have got Black Death then this could materially affect your social life. I think this is something you should discuss with your mortician.

CIRCUMCISION

Ritual circumcision raises a hotly-debated point – is the operation healthy or simply a barbaric rite? It owes its origins to peer-group identification in the Middle East and many sociologists regard it as the earliest form of passport. This is also true of circumcision in New York today. However, it also serves a socially cohesive purpose since not only is the circumcisee accepted as a man (albeit a teentsy bit less of a man) by the tribe, but the cicumcisor is similarly honoured, revered and rewarded. In this respect it represents a unique form of economic transaction, and some socio-economists have been able to construct a model of non-Keynesian café society that exists entirely by snipping bits off each other. The Labour Party is another example.

GALL-BLADDER

The gall-bladder is a sterile cul-de-sac on the broad highway of the bile duct. It is a relatively unlovely bag-shaped organ nestling in the shade of the liver (mind you, it's all pretty dark inside the abdomen – except during surgery – so 'shade' is a bit of poetic licence). The interesting thing is that when you are born your gall-bladder is empty but by the time you are middle-aged you've got a one-in-three chance of having stones in it. The Ancients puzzled over this phenomenon for centuries, thinking of it as the earliest form of 'locked-room' detective story, and Aristophanes wrote his comedy *The Stones* about it.

It was only in the Age of Enlightenment (1952–58) that research revealed that gallstones were actually made inside the gall-bladder. Why they are made there, how they are made there and for what purpose they are made is still unknown. Some biochemists blame stone-formation on a bile supersaturated with cholesterol in the presence of lecithin deficiency, whereas others blame it on the trade unions. Personally, I think it's a bit of both and would advise anyone with the slightest twinge of gall-bladder trouble to think seriously about joining the SDP (after all, it's run by a doctor *and* they take credit cards).

Glandology

As a doctor I've had absolutely tons of letters from people who think they are overweight because of their glands. Well, just occasionally they're absolutely right – one woman I know weighed seventeen stone and I was able to demonstrate to her sceptical husband (a steeplejack, and just as well) that in total nearly three stone of her weight consisted purely of glands. But what are glands, what do they do, how do they work and what colours do they come in? The answers are right here!

THE PITUITARY GLAND

The pituitary gland is a tiny sort of gland-shaped thing that sits in the middle of your brain behind your eyes where you can't see what it's doing. This is a problem since it does a large number of things including deciding how tall you're going to be, when (if ever) you're going to have puberty and whether or not you're going to grow a beard, breasts or feathers. The pituitary has been called the 'conductor of the endocrine orchestra' – and rightly so, since it is erratic, temperamental, and only works for about two days at a time. It has got several very important functions to do with fatness and obesity but I can't remember what they are. The back part or (you should excuse me) 'posterior' pituitary secretes stuff that decides how much urine you're going to pass though most people blame it on the beer.

The pituitary receives instructions from a more powerful gland called the 'hypothalamus' (from the Greek words meaning 'sleeping policeman') – so if the pituitary is the conductor of the orchestra, the hypothalamus is like the Arts Council. Between the two of them, these glands control all the most important aspects of human reproduction and fertility except booking the restaurant beforehand and lighting the cigarettes afterwards. Recent research by Harvard socio-endocrinologists has shown that pituitary control of testosterone (male hormone) release is the second largest cause of human misery apart from estate agents.

THE ADRENALS

These are two cap-shaped glands which sit like caps (hence their name which means something or other in Latin) on top of the kidneys or sometimes other giblets. They are the main originators of the 'fight-or-flight' reaction and are thus responsible for many things including Freddie Laker. In the cat the adrenals cause rising of the fur and snarling but in man they just cause contraction of the erector-pili muscles (for example in traffic jams) which creates a prickly feeling on the back of the neck and marital rows. The adrenals control blood pressure but not very well, so you need to see doctors as well.

The adrenals manufacture and pump out a substance called adrenalin, which should really be called adrenalout but isn't. Adrenalin or to give it its proper biochemical name 'monosodium glutamate' is a hormone which makes you nervous. Many hormones do this, particularly if you read about them. In excess, adrenalin can cause heart attacks but, if you believe what you read in the papers, so can everything else, so it's no great shakes after all. People who are said to 'live on their adrenalin' aren't telling the truth and usually keep chocolates in their desk.

THE THYROID

Everybody knows about the thyroid from folklore and old wives' tales, as in 'a lazy thyroid maks wee muckle' (Scotland) and 'all work and no thyrotrophic releasing hormone makes Jack a mesomorph' (England and Wales arr. Cecil Sharp). The thyroid sets the pace of the body's metabolism. For example, some people may be seriously lacking in thyroid and may become sluggish, and lethargic, getting puffy around the eyes and becoming very constipated – such people should go and see their doctor who will recommend a career in local government.

Spain
SPAIN
A walking holiday, please, but not France this time.
SPAIN
ITALY
CYPRUS
Minorca
Solitor
Italy
CANARY ISLANDS
MADE

The Pineal Gland Frogs take their summer holidays at the same time as we do

THE PINEAL GLAND

This is an extraordinary gland – it lives in the middle of your brain (as does the pituitary but in a more select area) and doesn't seem to do very much. However some very exciting research in frogs has shown that their pineal glands tell them when it's time to change colour and when the seasons are changing – personally I would have thought it would have been bleeding obvious to a cold-blooded animal diving nose-first onto an iced pond that winter had arrived, but it seems frogs need a whole gland for the job.

Anyway, when it comes to man, things are hardly better. No matter how clever we *think* we are, without our pineal gland pumping out hormones apparently we'd never be able to book a summer holiday on our own. Even more extraordinarily, biochemists have identified the pineal hormone in both frog and man; it's the same stuff exactly, which is why frogs take their summer holidays at the same time as we do. No one fully understands how man controls the pineal gland itself, but there is some evidence that it can be strongly inhibited by high concentrations of Ambre Solaire.

THE PARATHYROIDS

These are also rather fascinating glands, so named because they look so much prettier than the thyroid itself. They control the calcium in your blood if they feel like it. They are thus responsible for giving you strong bones and healthy teeth and a glossy coat and wet nose and many other things our mothers told us came from the greens that we didn't want to finish. The parathyroids cannot be seen in life because they're so small and also very shy. They don't come out at night (very few glands do) and are very difficult to measure, scan, assay and house-train. However if you take care of them, they will reward you with a loyalty unmatched in the endocrine system.

Jointology

Another thing (or things) that people who write to me about is (or are) rheumatism and arthritis and things like that – a group of conditions known in medicine as 'the rheumatic and arthritic conditions and things like that'. The same goes for the many complaints we all hear about 'cold in the bones' or 'old bones', particularly in the kind of restaurants I go to. Well I wish I could answer these inquiries, but unfortunately I was away on the Thursday they taught rheumatology, so we'll have to make do with a few basic facts about our bones and joints.

THE SKELETON

As some of you may know, the arthropods (eg lobsters, crabs, smoked salmon etc) have an *exoskeleton*: that is to say, the skeleton is on the outside of the body, which has the advantage that you can see it easily, and see if it's broken without getting X-rayed – though there are disadvantages to this arrangement as anyone who has tried to eat lobster thermidor in polite company while wearing a white shirt can tell you. Mankind, on the other hand, has an *endoskeleton*, with the bones inside the body, which has the advantage of keeping them dry when it rains. This could be quite important, I suppose, since bone is a very porous substance and easily soaks up aqueous solutions, as in soup.

Anyway, bone is basically a protein which is hardened and made rigid by getting smothered in calcium, which is terrifically useful when it happens to bones but not so good when it happens to coronary arteries. The most extraordinary thing about bone is that it's very light and very strong and it actually gets stronger when pressure is applied to it – a useful property that many other materials could benefit from, eg the pound sterling.

The Vertebrae There are 435 vertebrae in each rugger team, which accounts for the higher incidence of breakages

THE FEMUR

The femur is the thigh-bone and occurs in two main forms, the left and the right. Most people are born with one of each, which sounds easy but when you think of the number of times you buy kits for kitchen-units with two left-hinged doors it's actually a miracle. The femur (plural femora, neutral) is also the longest bone in the body, leading from the hip joint or acetabulum (from the Latin 'ace' and 'tabulum' meaning 'very nice table') to the knee. The femur is encased in a huge bulk of muscle, some of which is called the quadriceps, which means 'four-headed' which is precisely twice the number of heads found in the biceps muscle in the arm, which is why it's twice as easy to walk on your legs as walk on your hands.

THE PELVIS

The pelvis is composed of several bones called the ischium, the ilium, the sacrum, the fulcrum, the bathrum and the ballrum. The pelvis is shaped a bit like a bucket, and, just like a bucket, it provides a rigid container protecting the organs within (the womb, bladder, rectum, bedrum etc). However, in addition, it is part of the skeleton and transmits the forces of gravity upwards from the legs to the spine in exactly the same way a bucket doesn't. In its role as container, the pelvis protects the developing foetus inside the womb for the first nine months of existence until it is old enough to be made a ward of court.

The pelvis is held together with ligaments of which the most famous are ones at the back called the sacro-iliacs. These are a common cause of back-pain and disability, and a recent DHSS survey has shown that they are most likely to cause trouble in women during childbirth and in men the day before a Cup replay.

THE VERTEBRAE

In mammals the backbone is composed of a set of blocks called vertebrae balanced on top of each other. There are 29 vertebrae altogether in all mammalian species and 435 vertebrae in each rugger team, which accounts for the higher incidence of breakages. The vertebrae are separated from each other by plates of gristle called 'intervertebral discs'. Anatomists have known for generations that severe damage can occur if one vertebra slides off the disc, as can happen when you are hanged.

The disc itself consists of the outer annulus, the nucleus pulposus, the romulus and remus. It can be ruptured (discus herniatus), partially torn during exercise (discus interruptus), broken (disc breaks), sintered, blanched, diced or marinated. Osteopaths claim that none of these conditions can be improved by conventional methods, but then they would, wouldn't they? One way of preventing the pain and disability of a slipped disc is to spend your life lying down, never lifting anything heavier than a gin and tonic. This also has the advantage of preparing you for a career in advertising.

THE HUMERUS

There is nothing funny about the humerus.

THE MANDIBLE

The mandible is the lower jawbone which is the bit that moves when you talk and drops when you see the phone bill. The World Health Organisation named it Bone of the Year in 1983, when it remained the only part of the body not to be found guilty of sexism and was not ordered to change its name to persondible. The mandible is responsible for carrying the lower teeth, though when you think of the number of dental extractions each year, it obviously doesn't take its reponsibilities very seriously.

The front of the mandible is, of course, the chin, and cosmetically it often causes distress. However, a lot can be done to help. A chin that is thought to be too small can easily be accentuated, eg by sticking a violin under it. Or if it's very small, try a cello. For disguising a big chin, try growing a beard, although in adolescence many girls find this difficult and have to improvise with mascara and blusher. Most important of all, a big silly chin needn't be a bar to success – look at that marvellously brave Tony Benn, for example.

THE FEET

The feet are two lozenge-shaped organs situated at the bottom of the legs. There is normally a left one and a right one, and doctors still do not understand how a foetus developing in the womb 'knows' how to put the correct foot on the correct leg. Particularly as it's so dark in there. The bone structure of the foot is designed on a cantilever principle. This design evolved when our ancestors adopted erect posture and it enabled primitive man to transmit the full force of the body weight towards the front part of the foot, eg when kicking someone's head in. This explains why fossils of Peking Man show that the foot had evolved into its present shape before the evolution of the opposable thumb, deciduous teeth or steel toe-caps.

The foot became an object of worship and fetishism at an early stage and we know that the Ancient Greeks performed devotional acts at the shrines of the powerful goddess Dolcis. There are approximately 34 bones in the human foot and they usually get on together just fine, unless working conditions become extremely cramped and stressful as in ballet-shoes. Actually, ballet dancers have exceptionally well-developed big toes but everything else you hear about them is untrue.

THE KNEES

The knee is a pretty amazing thing, too. In functional terms it offers the leg the last chance to change direction after the hip before the ankle. The 'knobble' of the knee is caused by the knee-cap or 'patella', as it is known – or is that the rotten Spanish dish that looks like hot rice salad and tastes of fried pencil shavings? Anyway, the knee-cap or 'kedgeree' or whatever is situated in front of the knee joint itself, which means that it is very vulnerable to traumatic damage, particularly if you live in Italy and have strong views about things.

The most important feature of man's knee joint is that it is 'lockable' and capable of supporting the body without muscular effort for many hours – an ability we share with many other mammalian species, eg the police-horse. The knee reflex, which doctors produce with those fascinating rubber-covered, blunt instruments, is a useful test of the spinal nerves. It should strictly be called the 'patellar reflex' and the term 'knee jerk' should only be used to describe rich osteopaths. The front of the knee is protected by a fluid–filled bag called a 'bursa', which is Latin for 'bear', as in the galaxy Bursa minor which looks exactly like a knee-cap, or rather a bit like one if you squint at it and include a couple of stars from Andromeda.

Interestingly, the well-known disease 'housemaid's knee' was re-classified at the Zurich InterContinental Housemaid's Symposium last year. Recent studies have shown that the condition actually tends to affect males rather than females, outdoor occupations rather than indoor ones, and elbows, toes and groins rather than knees, and will thus be re-named 'athlete's foot'.

ELBOWS

The design of the elbow is very similar to that of the knee, particularly in the kind of suits that I buy. Like the knee, the elbow is a planar joint and will only allow movement in one direction except under very unusual circumstances, eg Indian wrestling. The way the muscles are attached around the elbow actually makes it a mechanically inefficient joint and difficult to control, which is why so many of us in polite company find it hard to drink a cup of tea without getting the spoon caught up the nose.

The back part of the elbow has a bursa of its own which can be chafed or irritated very easily – in fact, it is the most easily inflamed structure in the whole of human evolution apart from the South Americans. It is this inflammation of the bursa by various activities which causes the galaxy of specific complaints so loved in sports medicine. These include the so-called 'golfer's elbow', 'tennis elbow', 'spectator's elbow', 'adulterer's elbow', and 'policeman's elbow' (the accepted medical term for a truncheon).

One word of caution: there is an adage to the effect that you should 'never stick anything in your eye sharper than your elbow'. While this is commendable advice as regards the eye, it should be pointed out that you could only stick your own elbow in your eye if someone has pulled your arm off first.

WRISTS

The term 'wrist' is derived from the Old Norse word 'wreest' meaning a type of open sandwich. In fact almost all Old Norse words meant some kind of open sandwich, which is why the Norwegians were so lousy at poetry and so good at outside catering. A lot of nineteenth-century English literature of the most vigorous kind (ie smutty) mentioned the slimness and slenderness of women's wrists, and it certainly seems that in those days the wrist was an erogenous zone. As it still is today, particularly if you're getting desperate. In fact, slim wrists almost became a bit of a political issue, and last year the GLC Feminist Anatomists Against the Rest of the World Committee allowed the back of the wrist to be an erogenous zone provided it was declared nuclear-free.

The wrist is the nearest thing to a universal joint that nature has manufactured, or at least has in stock for immediate delivery. It can provide movement in two directions, eg up and down, and has thus enabled man to develop a complex vocabulary of hand gestures which depend heavily on a flexible wrist and a fast car.

Bugsology

As myself and any doctor will tell you, once you get out and about and start mingling with the wonderful ordinary people of this world, you'll catch an infection. Or several even. Now there have been lots of scares and panics recently, so here are a few reliable points for you. (*Note: despite the content of this chapter and public anxiety you will not catch anything from reading what follows. But do wear thick glasses to be on the safe side.*)

HEPATITIS

Hepatitis is a condition in which the liver becomes inflamed and it is caused by one of two viruses called Hepatitis A and Hepatitis B, though nobody knows which is which, including their mother. Hepatitis A is commoner and is transmitted in what we doctors call, you should pardon me, sewage. Hepatitis is often contracted by holidaymakers abroad because for the last 400 years the people of Southern Europe and Northern Africa have regarded the Mediterranean Sea as a vast chemical toilet which God hasn't yet taken away to empty.

However, the good news is that in the Mediterranean there lives a species of animal that spends its entire life lying on its back sucking in gallon after gallon of sewage-rich water and filtering out all the clag and crud, including the hepatitis. The bad news is that these animals are called mussels. The French have devised a way of dealing with this health hazard. They boil the infected mussels in salted water and serve them to the English. Other transmissible French diseases include rabies, typhus and balzac.

Hepatitis They boil the infected mussels in salted water and serve them to the English

CHICKEN-POX

In the Middle Ages it was thought that 'chicken-pox' could be transmitted by chickens. Nowadays we know that the only health hazard associated with chickens is if you eat the clean-up tissue thinking it's the barbecue sauce. In fact chicken-pox is a true 'pox', that is, its basic unit is a pustular vesicle called a 'pock' (which is why chickens go around saying pock-pock-pock all the time). Chicken-pox is (or more accurately 'are') caused by a virus called Herpes Zoster, which belongs to the same virus family as the one that causes genital herpes, though they never hear from *him* much nowadays since he's become so famous and popular.

The rash of chicken-pox resembles that of the once fatal disease smallpox, except that it is densest on the face and head. Sixteenth-century doctors knew how to distinguish chicken-pox from smallpox by coming back in two weeks and seeing if the patient was dead. Smallpox was so named to distinguish it from the Great Pox, also known as Samuel Johnson.

MUMPS

Mumps is a disease in which you often get painful swelling of the salivary glands (parotitis), and occasionally get swelling of the pancreas (pancreatitis), and testicles (orchitis, see *balzac* above). The name was coined from the Middle English word 'maump', meaning a painful lump, eg King John. The virus causing mumps is usually transmitted by droplet infection as in coughing or party political broadcasts. The incubation period of the disease is variable, ie I can't remember what it is, though to be on the safe side allow at least 28 days for delivery anywhere on the mainland. (I am over eighteen.) A recent survey of public attitudes towards infectious diseases in Idaho showed that 72 per cent of married women were afraid that mumps would render their husbands sterile and 18 per cent were afraid it wouldn't.

MEASLES

Measles, or rubeola, is one of a group of skin rashes which includes 'German' measles (rubella), 'Jewish' measles (rubenella), 'fish' measles (salmonella) and 'wet' measles (umbrella). The virus lives in the upper respiratory tract which is the posh way of saying up your nose. One of the earliest diagnostic signs of infection are the so-called 'Koplik spots' which look like little grains of salt inside the mouth. A word of caution here – there are other things that resemble grains of salt inside the mouth, and the most important of these are the so-called 'pseudo-Kopliks', which are caused by the actual presence of grains of salt inside the mouth. Particles of cheese 'n' onion crisps on the palate, tonsils, shirt and bedside table may clinch the diagnosis.

INFLUENZA

Extraordinarily enough, the disease of influenza was originally named after a person – the Influenza was the title traditionally given the second eldest daughter of the reigning monarch of Portugal and was derived from the Spanish for 'snotty nose'. Contrary to popular belief, during an attack of influenza most people do not suffer sneezes and coughs (which more often accompany the common cold). The usual symptoms are chills, fevers, shakes and a sense of malaise as when you get a parking ticket. Virologists in Salisbury have been able to show that for every person with the full-blown 'flu' there are ten people with a minor form (without the chills and shakes) and a thousand people with the mildest and subtlest form of all, in which nothing is wrong with them at all. This last condition may be reaching epidemic proportions, and if it does (or even has) nobody will be able to tell.

It has often been said that influenza only strikes when you're 'run down' and recently immunologists have been able to show that the old-fashioned feeling of being 'run down' is actually a reflection of depleted new-fashioned T-helper lymphocytes in the blood. Further research has shown that the commonest cause of depletion of T-helper lymphocytes is catching influenza. The flu virus changes its outer coat every few years and each epidemic is named after the place where the new coat was first detected – thus 'Asian' flu began in Kashmir, 'Red' flu began in Nishky-Novgorod, and 'Chinese' flu began in Gerrard Street.

Bladderology

All the time, we are told on the radio and television and in the newspapers about the government's difficulties with the balance of payments. Well, you may not realise it, but every minute of every day your own body is performing its own miraculous balance of payments: controlling the water and fluid content of the body. It monitors exports, eg of sweat, urine and tears, and balances this with the intake, ie drinking without any form of import restriction and at constant risk of the Japanese flooding the market. Here's how it does it.

THIRST & DRINKING

Drinking is a complex phenomenon which has baffled physiologists for years – which is why many of them have taken it up professionally. Basically, the thing that makes us drink is thirst (if you're unmarried) and this is controlled by the hypothalamus in the brain. There are three nerve centres involved. The first centre measures how concentrated the blood is and decides whether the body needs more fluid. The second centre decides what kind of fluid and how much the body needs. The third centre decides whether it's the body's turn to buy the next round. Then they all get together, order the drinks and immediately inhibit or 'override' all the rest of the cerebral cortex which is why nobody ever says anything intelligent in a pub. By this means, the sensation of thirst carefully controls the total amount of water in the body, except during drowning.

The brain also regulates fluid output, to some extent, by deciding how much urine should be passed, when, and (unless you're very drunk) where. It does this by sending out a hormone code-named ADH which acts on the kidneys by a mechanism that is either unknown or else cannot be revealed because of national security.

GENTS

Bladder Troubles Bagpipes are made from bladders – so if your bladder is giving you trouble, you can always threaten it with that

KIDNEYS

Kidneys are very similar in all mammals and consist of two bean-shaped organs situated (depending on the species) either at the back of the lower abdomen next to the adrenals, or on a bed of rice next to the mushrooms. They cleanse the blood by a filtration process, similar to a coffee-percolator but quieter. During the filtration, the kidneys hold back useful chemicals in the blood (glucose, salt, gold, diamonds etc) while simultaneously filtering out unwanted substances (urea, ammonia, polystyrene, empty bottles, odd socks etc). When you realise that the kidneys filter one litre of blood every minute, all the year round, with no overtime payments or prospects of promotion, you'll see why kidney transplants have been welcomed by the kidneys themselves, because at least it gives them a change of scenery.

The only important thing a kidney has to decide is whether a particular substance is wanted or unwanted and recent research from Cornell has shown that they 'decide' by using a process well-known in physiology called guesswork. The kidneys are vital to life since without them the brain would not function, the blood would turn acid, and steak-and-kidney pie would be even duller.

THE BLADDER

The bladder is an unloved and unlovely organ which takes in a continuous stream of urine and releases it in regular dollops, just like the *News of the World.* As the bladder fills up or distends, it stimulates stretch receptors in the walls and in the waistband of the underpants. These send signals to the brain requesting emptying of the bladder. The brain ignores these signals until a certain point, which in seven-year-old children is the sign saying 'No Services on Motorway for 30 miles' and in adults is when the dentist says 'next please'.

The reflex emptying of the bladder involves autonomic nerves, causes contraction and relaxation of over forty non-striated muscles and usually contravenes fifteen bye-laws, particularly in swimming pools. During the winter months when we sweat very little and the air is cold, the bladder empties frequently and the urine is relatively dilute, but during the summer we lose much more fluid in sweat and evaporation, so bladder-emptying is needed less frequently (which is the excuse the council gives for not providing enough toilets at the seaside).

BLADDER TROUBLES

Bladder troubles can afflict both sexes, and particularly men and women. The commonest is the inflammation called 'cystitis' which gets its name from '-itis' which means 'inflammation' and the Latin 'cystoe-' which means 'makes your eyes water'. Cystitis is commoner in women and can be precipitated by mechanical trauma within the pelvis – eg caused by mechanics or other rough trade. There is thus the well-known holiday phenomenon called 'honeymoon cystitis' (although reputable travel agents can insure you against it).

Men's bladders are less prone to honeymoon cystitis, though not for lack of trying, and are more prone to problems caused by the prostate gland. This gland sits under the bladder and its sole function is to impede bladder-emptying like a grouchy policeman on point duty. It can be removed surgically (unlike policemen) and serve it right, too. It's always worth remembering that bagpipes are actually made from bladders, so if yours is giving you trouble, you can always threaten it with that.

THE DOCTOR ANSWERS YOUR QUESTIONS

Q: What are anabolic steroids?

A: I have honestly no idea. Unless you're thinking of Anna Bolicsteroids, the cello-playing sister of famous sportsman Severiano Bolicsteroids?

Bloodology, Sweatology and Tearsology

In this chapter I'd like to take a frank and honest look at some of the body's more interesting secretions; those fluids emanating from eye, mouth, nostril and armpit which help to make life flow more smoothly. And also that valuable biological resource, blood – which shouldn't be emanating from any of the aforementioned. So let's not be prudish but learn a little about the human body's 'liquid assets'. And about some of the places they're found coming out of from.

RED BLOOD CORPUSCLES

The red blood corpuscles are the things that give blood its characteristic cheerful colour and they are extremely small, which I suppose is why it's so difficult to get blood stains out. Actually they are so small that in one litre of blood you get five *million million* of them (and that's retail – you can get over six million million for wholesale). What they do is travel to the lungs were they pick up several molecules of oxygen and then go via the heart to various organs, eg kidneys, brain, tripe, nose, hanky etc. There they exchange the oxygen for the same amount of carbon dioxide, or for a voucher of similar value. Corpuscles can be penalised for dropping molecules, swearing or taking dope and may be disqualified or forced to go round again.

What makes the corpuscles look red is stuff called haemoglobin (from the Greek words 'haemo' meaning 'looks like blood' and 'globin' which means '*is* blood'). Now haemoglobin, like its sister molecules myoglobin and dunglobin, contains a lot of iron. This is why children need to eat food with lots of iron, eg spinach, though personally I have never understood why parents force babies to eat spinach, which they don't like, and yet stop them eating other iron-containing foods which they do like, eg rust.

WHITE CELLS

The white cells in the blood are like the policemen of the body's defence system and, like policemen, have a great tendency to be somewhere else when you want them, eg if you've got a pimple coming. There are actually many different kinds of white cells, although they are all white, which makes them easy to distinguish from the red, of which there is only one type, ie red. And personally, I think the same applies to Spanish wine. Anyway, white cells whizz around the bloodstream attacking invaders like bacteria and viruses and harassing other potentially harmful pathogens such as protozoa, students and squatters.

When a foreign substance or 'antigen' establishes itself inside your body, like for instance if you're stabbed with an assegai, then the white cells recognise this (and so they bloody well should) and are attracted to the site by a process called 'chemotaxis'. Mind you, a fat lot of use they are when they get there; what you really need is a shield, or better still a gun. Some white cells are called 'lymphocytes' and these are the cells responsible (according to the prosecution) for allergies and reactions. Conversely, allergens are defined as substances which have the ability to provoke major reactions in the vast majority of normal individuals. Robert Maxwell is a good example.

PLATELETS

Platelets are little particles in the blood that help it clot when it comes into contact with unexpected substances, eg air. Their name simply means 'little plates' which, seeing as how they are less than one hundred-thousandth of an inch across, is a bit of an understatement even if you're talking about a doll's tea-set. Platelets are full of complex glycolipids and prostaglandin-activators which can perform a very large number of intricate and crucial biochemical procedures, but I simply can't remember one of them. So if you want to know more ask the tea-lady at the transfusion centre.

PLASMA

Plasma is the straw-coloured fluid that all the cells slosh around in. It contains most of the nutrients necessary to sustain life and you can get the rest from Safeway. The problem with plasma is that it has to carry anything that gets into it (just like a London taxi, really) including alcohol, poisons, drugs, dope, sex, long hair and many other symptoms of a degenerate society. Because plasma is so rich in protein and can carry a little oxygen, it is very useful as a substitute for real blood when a person has lost a lot of blood and requires a transfusion. Other volume-expanders such as dextrans can also be used, and some alternative doctors have recently found a way of replacing plasma with a non-protein non-toxic ecologically valid crystalloid solution called camomile tea.

BLOOD GROUPS

Blood groups are the haematological equivalent of racial prejudice. They allow the body's defence system (ie policemen, see above) to recognise blood cells of another group and, using immunologically active plasma components, to beat the backside off them. The first type of blood group to be discovered was the ABO system in which types A and B are incompatible with each other (and usually married to each other), and type O has the lowest tendency to provoke a transfusion reaction and is called the 'universal donor', like Nubar Gulbenkian for instance. Then came the Rhesus groups in which Rhesus-positive was found to be incompatible with Rhesus-negative, then came the Lewis groups, then the Betamax, then the Grundig system which turned out to be incompatible with everything.

Combinations of blood groups vary considerably in the population – thus a combination of Group A and Rhesus-positive is fairly common, whereas B-Rhesus-negative is so rare that people possessing this blood group can get a grant from the GLC Minorities Committee. In America, self-awareness has now reached the level of molecular biology and people of the same blood group get together in blood-group support groups to examine their attitudes and share their problems and transfusion requirements. Among the Americans, the commonest type of blood is Republican.

SALIVA

Saliva is produced by the salivary glands, of which there are three pairs situated inside the cheeks. These produce saliva and pump it into the mouth by a process that scientists call 'dribbling'. Things that start people dribbling are called 'stimuli' (in mixed company) and they work in different ways. For instance, lemon juice acts by a completely involuntary reflex action to produce salivation (unless it goes in the eye by mistake). Whereas more complex stimuli require you to have some experience to start the dribbling (eg looking at a picture of a lemon) whilst the highest order of visual stimuli can produce reflex dribbling only after much learning and conditioning, eg a Pirelli calendar.

The name 'saliva' came into use during the eleventh century to honour the Italian mystic, Frederico Saliva of Pepperone, the patron saint of drooling, who was martyred by militant vegetarians outside a sausage shop. The main object of saliva is to lubricate food to make it easier to swallow, and a variety of other natural fluids perform the same function, eg wine. Saliva also contains enzymes which break down starches and other carbohydrates, which is why your shirt goes floppy when other people spit on it. Microbiologists have known for centuries that the touch or sight of certain salivas can be dangerous, and this list includes rabid dogs, vampires and Nigel Lawson.

SWEAT

Sweat is much more than a nuisance, it is actually a complex biological signal. Some animals, including man, have developed complex subtle signalling systems such as spoken language, courtship dances, and singles bars. In these species, sweat has only a vestigial function and, in man, profuse sweating serves the biological function of signalling to members of the opposite sex that the person is a sweaty person. However, in the anthropoid apes, eg gorillas, marmosets, estate agents etc, the composition of sweat is incredibly variable and is materially affected by the weather, hormonal state, sexual arousal, Dow Jones Index and proximity to David Attenborough.

The sexual signals in sweat are called pheromones and biochemists in Boston have discovered that the most powerful neutraliser of the female-attracting pheromones in human sweat is a substance called after-shave. When sweat is produced in response to a stressful or unpleasant stimulus, eg Robin Day, it becomes more acid and less viscous than usual, contains less sodium and has the specific property of glinting when the TV cameras are on it. Dr Conrad Lorenz has called this particular biological signal 'flop-sweat' and has shown that, in geese and ducks, it is associated with a sudden fall in peer-group precedence in the pecking order and with loss of privilege, premature senility and a job in local radio.

NOSE-PICKING DRIVER NO HAND SIGNALS
WUT 173

Nostrils Man is the only species in the animal kingdom
that picks his own nose while driving a car

Excessive sweating or 'hyperhidrosis' used to be regarded as a social disadvantage and in extreme cases could be treated with injections or surgery. However, health-consumer group therapists in Los Angeles now believe that this is an example of negative attitudes and poor self-image. They try to persuade very sweaty people that they are actually extremely lively, outgoing and attractive, but it's difficult to get the group members close enough to discuss it in detail.

TEARS

Tears also serve as biological signals but in addition have the important job of protecting the eye from damage by potentially dangerous and irritating stuff that it may encounter, like *Crossroads.* Tears are actually very powerful in many respects. For a start they contain a powerful bactericidal material called lysosyme which kills 94 per cent of facial germs and forces the remaining 6 per cent to seek political asylum in the left nostril. Secondly, tears produced as a result of an emotional conflict are a strong signal of submission, and Tinbergen has shown that among the black-headed gulls of Iceland when a female starts crying it usually ends up with the male building an extension to the nest and putting up the shelves he's always promised or getting her a new hat or something.

Recently, however, crying has changed from being the exclusive prerogative of the female. Due to changes in the perception of the stereotyped 'macho man' it has become possible for men to be virile, rugged and protective while they are also caring, sensitive and capable of blubbing away like a burst hydrant. Ernest Borgnine is a good example of this. This is typical of the way in which fixed signals can be reinterpreted by society to have the exact opposite meaning of that which was first intended. Other examples include 'the National Health Service is safe in our hands'.

MUCUS

Mucus is a biological resource which is ubiquitous, versatile, hard-working and useful in very many ways whilst appearing aesthetically unappealing, like Bernard Falk. Now you might think that mucus is only produced by glands situated up the nose, but this is a myth put about by manufacturers of paper hankies. In fact, mucus is produced in many places including the main bronchi, the stomach, the colon,

the Balearics and in some parts of Yorkshire, though the NUM are disputing the figures.

Mucus owes its viscosity to molecules called mucopolysaccherides which gang together in long chains and stick to dry surfaces, which is why they are pulled through ordinary tissues for men by their attraction to the palm of your hand. Mucus, like tears and sweat, is produced in response to irritating obnoxious substances, though slugs produce the stuff without any provocation at all. It has been suggested that during a sneeze, small droplets of mucus can reach speeds of 120mph due to the aerodynamic shape of the nostril, and that this is what gave the designers the idea for the Ford Sierra.

NOSTRILS

Thanks to the amazing power of evolution in producing erect posture and the brilliantly adaptable human hand, Man is the only species in the animal kingdom that can pick his own nose. Man is also the only species that almost always picks his own nose while driving a car. This would simply not be possible if, for instance, evolution had produced nostrils that point upwards, since Man's arm would then seriously impair his forward vision.

Contrary to popular supposition, picking your nose does not actually damage the brain unless your fingernails are four inches long and razor sharp. However, experiments with laboratory rats (who had to have their noses picked for them) have shown that the act of nasal excavation causes the release of a so-called 'pleasure hormone'. This hormone, which contains a great deal of glucose, fructose and galactose, is known as '4-hydro-peroxy-picknose' and is the most addictive substance known to science apart from Space Invaders. This is what makes it so difficult to stop the excavation, even if you're seen doing it when you stop at the traffic-lights.

In sociological terms, carrying on with the exploration while being watched is signalling to the person observing you that you are more interested in the contents of your own nose than in the opinion of the observer. Many people feel the same way about TV critics.

The Ears The ear-lobe is also a sensitive erogenous zone

THE EARS

The ears are pretty amazing things, too. For a start it is not generally realised that they are much more than simple organs for hearing. They actually have five functions. Apart from hearing, the external bit of the ear acts as a source of heat-loss, preventing heat-stroke while on holiday. The bottom of it or 'ear-lobe' is also a sensitive erogenous zone though not as much as you'd like, in my experience. The canal (or meatus or 'ear-hole') produces wax, a unique biological resource which can be thought of as an alternative source of energy during hibernation or power cuts. The inner ear performs many functions to do with balance, but I can't remember what they are.

Looking at the ears comparatively, human ones are relatively insensitive to high-frequency sounds compared to the ears of the bat, but look better in ear-rings. Camels can actually close their ears during a sand-storm. The muscles responsible for this do not exist in humans so we just have to pretend that we're not listening during an argument.

THE LIPS

Lips – like nostrils, eyes, kidneys, breasts and socks – are preferable in pairs. Thus man has an upper and a lower lip. Some species, such as the rabbit, have two upper lips or it looks like that anyway. Other species such as the elephant have virtually no upper lip at all which is why they are so unpleasant to kiss. For thousands of years, the lips have been decorated as part of tribal recognition patterns and Man is the only species that uses lipstick correctly, though it's fascinating to see what chimpanzees do with it if they get the chance.

Lips are thought to contain over seven hundred and fifty separate muscles needed for speech, smiling, snarling, puckering, blowing raspberries etc, and this is why they are the first organs to go badly wrong when you're getting drunk.

Allergyology

Allergies seem to be ever so common these days, don't they? Yes. In fact more and more people are claiming that they are allergic to lots of things – a few even believe that they are allergic to the twentieth century. Which is a shame because the twentieth century is the only one we've got in stock right now.

Just to set the record straight, here's a run-down on the whole field of immunology and thing. Allergies.

ALLERGIES

Allergies are abnormal reactions to substances that are not normally caustic. Thus you can't call it an allergy if the substance causes irritation or inflammation to everybody, eg sulphuric acid, rush hour, Nicholas Parsons etc. And of course there are substances which are too simple at a molecular level or too bland to cause any reaction, eg water, tapioca, Cliff Michelmore etc. In between are the materials that cause reactions in some people and not in others and which may – as we shall see – be the cause of these (eg Benny Hill).

However, the word 'allergy' is used very loosely by many people who really mean that they have a phobia ('I'm allergic to Thursdays'), although the difference can become academic. For example, some people are so phobic about work in any form that they become genuinely ill when confronted with any type of work, occupation or gainful employment. Such people cannot be cured by anti-allergic medicines or tablets, and have to be given a job in television.

HAY FEVER

Hay fever is an allergy to pollen and, to put it simply, pollen is what happens when grass wishes to have babies. Hay fever results from raiding-parties of pollen landing on the beachheads of your nostrils despite withering fire from air support, ie sneezes. When you think of how most plant seeds can grow in very adverse and hostile environments, eg Millwall, you realise that sneezing serves a purpose – ie if it weren't for hay fever we'd all have dandelions growing up our noses.

Since pollen grains are very small relative to noses, the best treatment is to prevent contact between pollen and nostril. Nowadays, this can be done in several simple ways, eg wearing a gas-mask or living in a submarine. I was once told that in the eighteenth century people sometimes had their nostrils bricked in, but maybe this wasn't to cure hay fever but to avoid the dreaded nostril tax, I can't remember. Anyway, that's where we get the phrase still used to this day, particularly by allergologists in Harley Street, 'hay fever sufferers pay through the nose'.

FOOD ALLERGIES

Many people claim to be allergic to various foods, additives or colourings used in modern restaurants, but immunologists from Carlisle have found that only one in ten of these is genuine. The other nine just want to get out of paying for their share of the meal. The problem is that genuine food allergies can produce many different symptoms, and sufferers claim that food allergies are the cause of their diarrhoea, stomach pains, headaches, depression, parking offences, minor embezzling and break dancing. The commonest foods associated with genuine allergies are peanuts, shellfish, strawberries and monosodium glutamate ('Chinese restaurant headache'). Interestingly, about 10 per cent of the giant man-eating clams of the Amazon get a headache and rash after eating Chinamen, although none of them are hungry an hour later.

I would advise caution before pleading a food allergy as the cause of behavioural problems. My friend Trevor was arrested in Mexico for being drunk and disorderly, and claimed that it was an allergic reaction to the Maraschino cherries in his pina coladas. The arresting officer beat the hell out of him and then blamed the violence on a hypersensitive reaction to his chewing gum.

SKIN ALLERGIES

A skin allergy is called 'eczema' if it occurs on elbows, ears, knees or bank holidays, and is called 'dermatitis' if it occurs on a private patient. Skin allergies can be caused by contact with rubber (eg gloves and tyres, particularly if run over by a lorry), with nickel (eg 'copper' coins, or suspenders if you're lucky), with gold (but who cares) and with funguses and mosses (eg Gray's allergy in a country churchyard).

Skin reacts to allergic stimulation by becoming inflamed and itchy and this initiates the reflex of scratching which makes the inflammation and itching worse. Nature presumably justifies this on the grounds of productivity. Doctors can tell which substances are causing the allergy by 'patch testing' in which pieces of the suspected material are kept in prolonged contact with the skin, a handy thing to remember if you're ever caught wearing ladies' suspender belts in your hat.

Another important thing to remember is that skin allergies can develop after years of trouble-free use of the allergen. One patient of mine developed a multiple allergy after ten years to mascara, lipstick, blusher toner and hair lacquer and it got so bad he had to resign his job at the Foreign Office.

THE DOCTOR ANSWERS YOUR QUESTIONS

Q: I'm very conscious of my lips and worried that there might be something wrong with them. Is there anything I can do?

A: Look at your lips now and ask yourself these questions: How many of them are there? Is there one above and one below the mouth? What colour are they? Do they meet when you say 'mmm'? If the answer to all these is 'yes', then you haven't read the questions properly. In general, lips will be more attractive and desirable if they don't move while you read.

Spring Cleaningology

It happens every year as the natural world unlocks after the imprisonment of winter – yes, spring or as the geophysicists call it, 'the venereal equinox'. Yet few people reflect that, as they begin the ritual of spring-cleaning, their own bodies need the odd spring-clean too. Here's how. And let's hope it's of some use to Mother Nature's very own branch of Sketchley's.

CLEANING THE MOUTH

The human mouth is full of many different important structures that require cleaning. They are called teeth. They are important because in the early days of man's evolution, someone who lost their teeth through decay would be unable to feed themselves and would starve before finding a mate, and would thus become extinct. Since bad breath is caused by plaque and tooth decay, we may legitimately regard halitosis as Evolution's first oral contraceptive.

The worry is that nobody really knows the best way of cleaning teeth. Some oral hygienists recommend fluoride-containing pastes used with a natural bristle brush, whereas most seven-year-old children recommend biscuits. Whatever the exact method, one has to remember that there are certain places where your toothbrush cannot reach, eg your kidneys. On the other hand, if your teeth do fall out, modern oro-faciomaxillary surgeons would suggest that the best thing you can do is to put them under your pillow and hope you get sixpence from the tooth-fairy.

Dental floss is a pretty good thing really, though it is a bit difficult to get rid of afterwards and if you try and flush it down the toilet, it can become a health hazard by staying there and making people think they've got tapeworms.

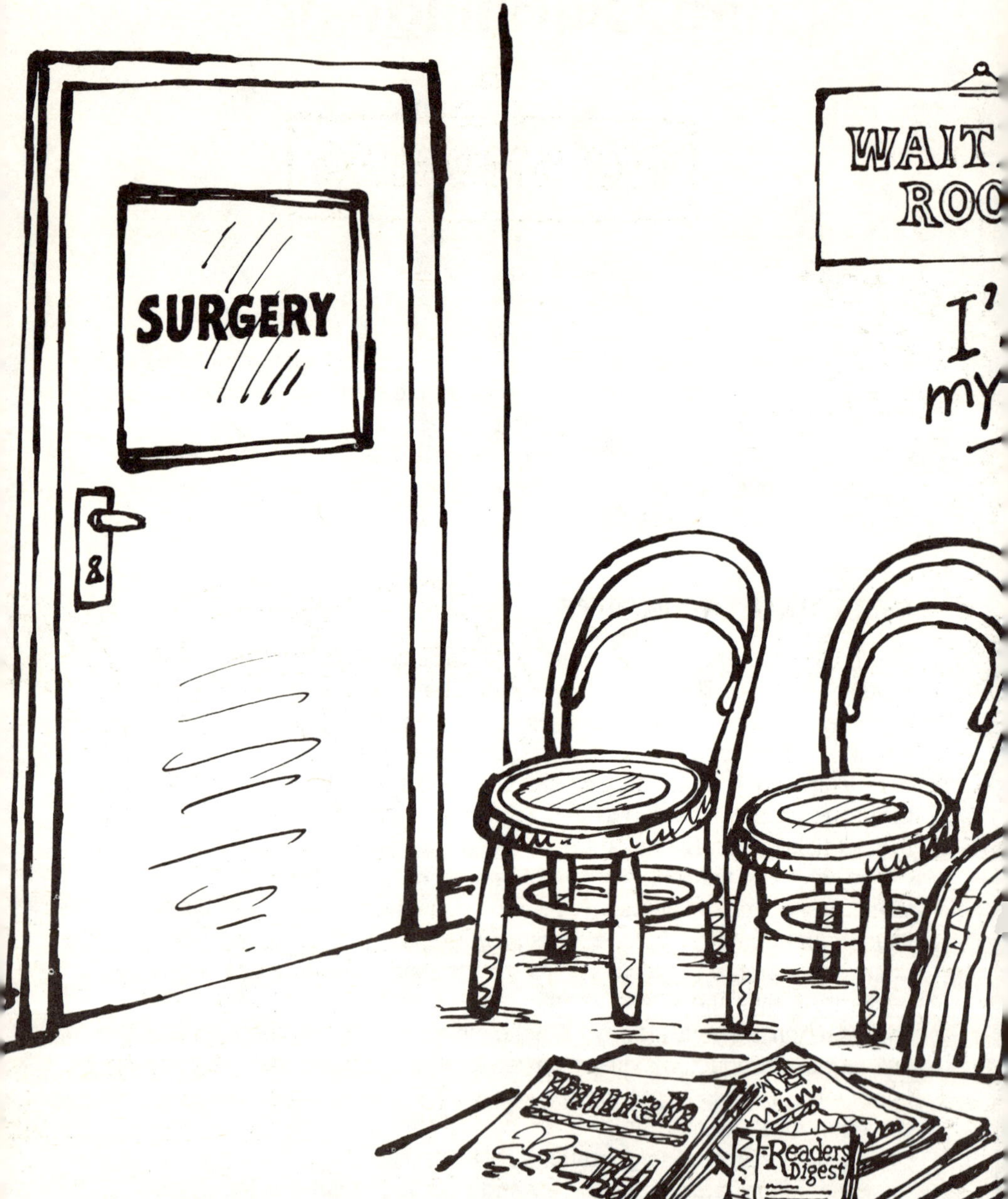

Cleaning the Mouth Halitosis: Evolution's first oral contraceptive

NO SMOKING
ere for
itosis
d you?....
PRIVATE EYE

CLEANING THE SKIN

The skin of all mammals is a growing, self-renewing and self-repairing organ. However, some factors are known to reduce these self-repairing properties, eg being made into a pigskin briefcase. In Man, the skin is also self-cleaning, although it's a bit slap-dash about it, particularly at the back of the neck and those parts that the dermatologists call the 'sock areas'. The problem is that the skin is an ecological playground for zillions of different bacteria which degrade skin proteins, producing many important biochemical by-products, all of which smell dreadful. However, frequent treatment of the skin with harsh soaps, detergents and disinfectants may destroy these bacteria and, although removing the smell, may leave the skin less pliable, more fragile and thinner, which is all right if you happen to be an egg but a worry otherwise.

For that reason, speaking as a doctor, I recommend that patients should wash their skin thoroughly and properly only when absolutely necessary, ie before coming to see me. At all other times, for best results, I suggest a quick wipedown with a non-abrasive material, eg salad oil or glycerol (anti-freeze will do), followed by gentle patting with absorbent materials, eg alpaca or peacock feathers, a quick dust with borax or carborundum and buffing with an ecologically valid substance, eg Brigitte Bardot. Do not wring.

CLEANING THE GUT

The gut or bowel measures over sixty feet in length from top to bottom and does not require much cleaning, which is just as well, since even with dental floss it would be a bit tricky, as well as rather unappetising to watch. Nature has designed many 'built-in' features to clean the gut in its various sections. For example, there is a fascinating mechanism by which the stomach-lining can be cleaned and freed of toxins, impurities and similar irritants. It's called being sick.

Lower down the gut, there is a great deal of mythology and faddism about the bowel habit. Most of it is nothing but hot air. It is not a good idea to worry about cleaning out the lower bowel, any more than it is a good idea to chromium-plate your dustbins. Unless, of course, you're trying to impress your neighbours. But then, very few neighbours want to look at your lower bowel anyway – except in certain areas of San Francisco.

The general message is leave well alone, though I have heard of some gurus in India who can control their perineal muscles so well that they can sit in a bowl of water and perform the rectal equivalent of gargling. I can't remember why they do this, but I'm told that, despite their extravagant claims of self-purification and inner enlightenment, this activity is still liable for entertainment tax.

CLEANING THE AIR

You may not realise it, but before the air you breathe actually gets into your lungs, it is thoroughly processed by the linings of your nose and upper airways. This is quite literally a form of biological 'air-conditioning' only less noisy. The airways are lined with mucus membranes covered with tiny hairs called 'cilia'. These linings take cold, dirty air, and they warm it, filter it, moisten it, starch it, press it and fold it, delivering it to the lungs in ready-to-use form (Bank Holidays excepted).

When the air contains particles of eg cigarette smoke, dust, clinker, sea-dredged aggregates etc, these will be trapped by the cilia which discolour with the process (hence 'cilia black') and then react by kicking the particles back up the airways in the form of a supra-critical, semi-morphous, colloidal suspension known to physiologists as 'snot'. When you think of the importance of getting clean air into the actual lung tissue, it is not surprising that the body is so good at getting rid of excess particulate matter which is why we so often find that snot is quite a handful.

THE DOCTOR ANSWERS YOUR QUESTIONS

Q: My dermatologist says I have a tendency to accumulate excessive oil. Should I do anything about it?

A: The tendency to accumulate oil can be a health hazard and may affect normal functions, particularly if you're a beach. If it's really excessive, the coastguard can spray you with detergent, but if it continues, it's probably worth accepting it and joining OPEC.

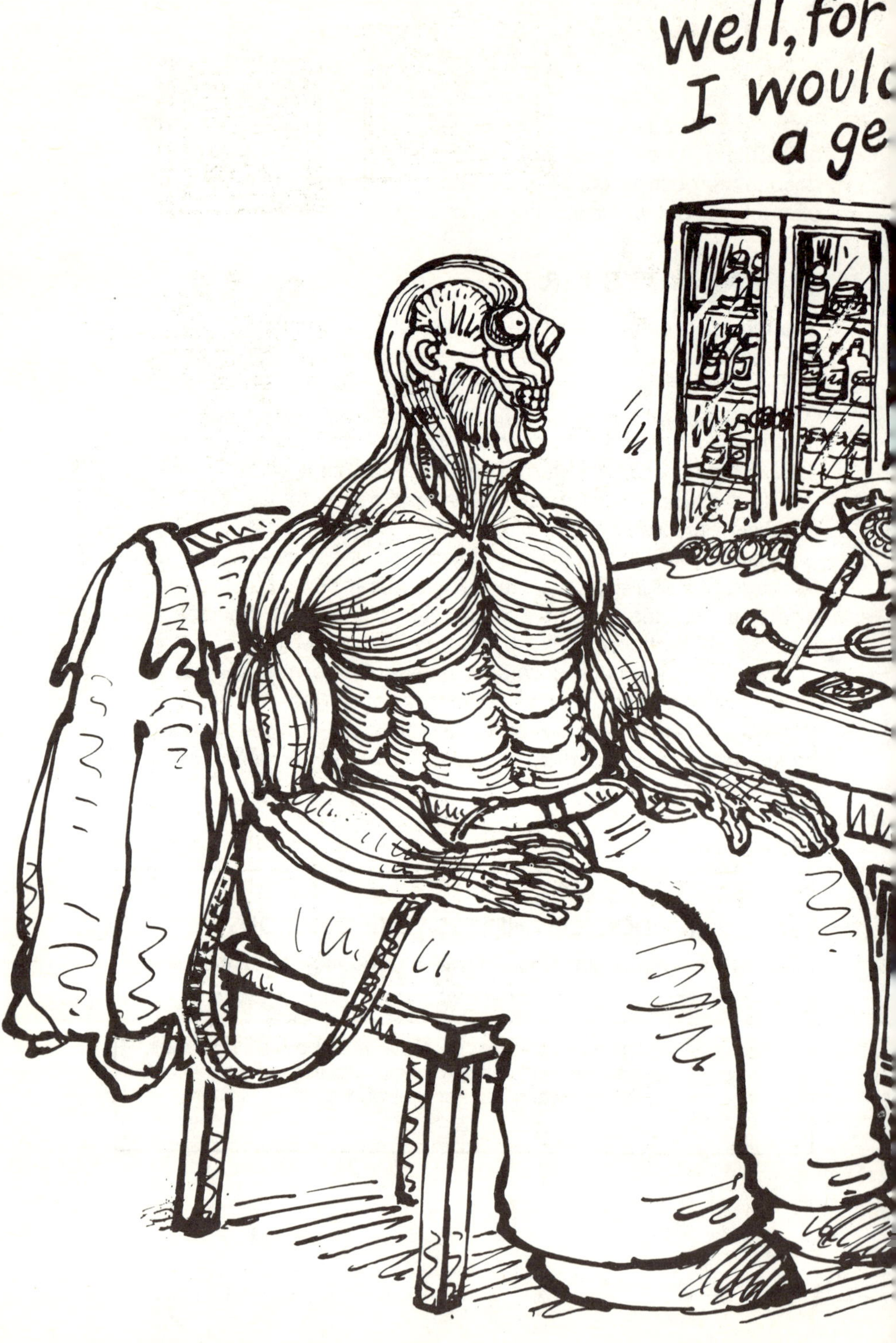
Well, for
I woul
a ge

Cleaning the Skin I recommend that patients should wash their skin thoroughly before coming to see me

Futurology

The future lies ahead. As it always has. But what does next year hold for us (apart from twelve more months)? Well, my own feeling is that the medical keynote of next year will undoubtedly be health scares and horrors. Probably. New discoveries by scientists (and some of their unsuspecting close contacts) will prove beyond a shadow of doubt that the things we all used to believe were good for us are actually lethal. Or worse.

Here are my predictions – and just remember that this is where you heard them first. Or rather read them (unless someone is reading this book out loud for you). You have been warned.

JANUARY

Bad start to the year when scientists in California show that jogging is a major cause of baldness. Great relief when 'jogger's baldness' is traced to a new virus of the Coxsackie group named *Alopeciavirus runna runna.* Vaccination against baldness promised by February. New wave of depression when discovered that the virus lives and multiplies inside tracksuits. Great relief when Salk Institute pioneer new way of vaccinating tracksuits.

Worse news mid-January: mineral water causes impotence. Health-conscious America immediately switches back to rye, Southern Comfort etc, only to find that the strain of avoiding mineral water because it might cause impotence, causes impotence. Coffee still suspect of causing something unpleasant in the region of the giblets, tea thought to cause dandruff. End of January sees massive transatlantic advertising campaign enhancing macho virile image of Ovaltine.

FEBRUARY

New panic when Ovaltine implicated in outbreak of green monkey disease. Panic subsides when Indianapolis zoologists point out that monkey is always green, which is why it is called green monkey, and is not disease at all. Panic breaks out again when visiting scientist from Tucson points out that this monkey wasn't green a week ago, therefore is disease. Panic subsides when visiting executives point out that green monkey, whether diseased or not, hasn't been drinking Ovaltine. Panic breaks out again when monkey discovered drinking Southern Comfort.

Feminist Psychologists Up Against The Wall Action Group (registered charity) publish extraordinary research work in field of neuro-endocrinology. This shows that sexual harassment at work actually causes degeneration of brain of harasser. Proves beyond doubt that the act of desiring to harass females causes release of 4,6 di-phenotestosterotrimphone into brain (if lucky). This material causes relentless loss of intellectual capacity and short-term memory which progresses slowly (over the whole afternoon) and may be fatal in less than fifty years. Disease found to be contagious and christened Sexual Harassment Related Encephalopathic Demyelination Syndrome or SHREDS. First SHREDS Self Help Group founded in Atlanta but measures to stop sexual harassment by self-help are declared illegal.

In Europe, centralisation of minor-surgery waiting-lists in Dusseldorf causes average wait for haemorrhoidectomy to be increased to seventy-one years. Causes formation of first ever EEC pile mountain.

THE DOCTOR ANSWERS YOUR QUESTIONS

Q: Just lately, I've had some very funny thoughts come into my mind, and the one that keeps on coming back is the feeling that I'm slowly turning into a set of matching vinyl travel luggage.

A: Get a grip on yourself.

MARCH

Himalayas suddenly found to be major cause of nose-bleeds. Campaign Against Nasal Blood Sports demands flattening of Himalayas to avoid further outbreaks. Questions in Parliament, K. Joseph unsympathetic to anti-bleeders, backed up by Lord Whitelaw supporting hunting, shooting and nose-bleeding set. N. Kinnock supports nose-bleeders but only up to a point.

New studies on sexual dominance published. Sociologists from Albany studying hamsters living in mixed colonies in over-crowded conditions discover that the reason why males become dominant and bossy and why females do washing-up, mending, Hoovering etc is all due to trousers. Contact of trousers enclosing legs causes secretion of pheromones from skin which induce obedience and submissive behaviour in females of same set. Proved that this applies to humans with daring experiment in House of Representatives when bossy dominant behaviour is abolished by removal of trousers. Pan American Trousers Inc employs sixty biochemists to find out exactly what constituent of trousers causes most obedience. Government buy extract for military use.

Ginseng found to be major cause of flat feet.

APRIL

New research in prostaglandins which are little chemical messengers involved in inflammation and causation of pain ('nature's little bringers of bad news'). Prostaglandins now shown to be involved in arthritis, in panniculitis and in the Brinks-Mat robbery. Prostaglandins plead sixteen other lysosomal functions at the organelle level to be taken into consideration and are let off with a caution.

Alternative medicine school moves into ante-natal care. Massive publicity for alternative medicine childbirth (using sea-salt, dried figs, coriander seeds and catching baby in a wok).

Falling populations in city centres cause central hospitals to be under-funded. City councils announce new schemes to get particular diseases adopted and sponsored by big organisations to stop them dying out. The common cold is adopted by Hitachi. Childbirth is sponsored by Aiwa. Patrick Jenkin adopts water on the knee.

MAY

Huge new pharmaceutical company scare. New antibiotic released as competitor to penicillin, amoxicillin and ampicillin. Is bright yellow capsule with red and purple stars and pink stripes. Is called reallycillin. Has only been released six weeks when new animal data showed that out of twenty laboratory mice, six died on reallycillin. Panic is resolved when discovered mice died when a crate of the capsules fell on them. De-luxe version of reallycillin capsule released with programmable remote control. Can be moved upwards to combat tonsillitis, downwards for gastro-enteritis, or in a circle from brain to rectum for party political broadcasts.

Belgium is found to be a major cause of depression.

JUNE

America faces first ever doctor shortage. US Defence dept deeply worried about implications for US Forces Casualties in event of war. Eventually ask Congress to fund the revolutionary MX-MEDIX programme in which one doctor will be concealed in seventy miles of tunnels with hundreds of dummy doctors (known as 'dermatologists') pushed around from place to place to confuse the public. Defence Dept are told that this is what most American hospitals are like anyway. Big international epidemiological survey comparing disease incidences in Europe and Asia proves conclusively that Switzerland is a major cause of getting old.

JULY

New virulent strain of Rocky Mountain Spotted Fever discovered. New strain of causative organism causes geographically limited endemic outbreak of non-haemorrhagic rhinitis. Is named Putney High Street Runny Nose but despite good reviews ('this rhinitis will run and run' – *Br J Infect. Dis.*) totally fails to catch on. Re-launch planned for September when may gain from increased consumer interest associated with the new season's influenza strains.

Ginseng found to be contributory cause of sunburn.

Sexual harassment plague SHREDS is shown not to exist at all – is merely wishful thinking on part of harassed neuro-endocrinologists. All get research grants into further methods of preventing sexual harassment: six of them learn karate, four practise voodoo and the other two try eating garlic-and-brie haddock quiche.

AUGUST

Good news. Major Californian survey shows that oral sex damages nothing except the art of conversation.

Ginseng found to cause short-sightedness and flaky nail syndrome.

Extraordinary preliminary results from Dickley Park Research Centre reported in *Daily Mail* show that hyper-acidity does no damage at all and may actually be associated with longer life. Fuller reports in *The Guardian* show that this only applies if you happen to be a car-battery.

Alternative medicine practitioners deeply upset with all the major side-effects of ginseng. Produce a substance which induces tranquillity and relaxation, is said to help release the inner being and enhance life-consciousness. This substance is called Valium. Hippy colony in Andover closes down when everyone gets sick smoking Valium.

SEPTEMBER

Season of mellow fruitfulness. Particularly true of bronchitis. New strain of Putney High Street Runny Nose is re-packaged as Dalston Junction Chesty Cough but suffers setback when fails to get distribution by EMI.

Picket-line violence between striking workers and police is investigated by Medical Research Council. Is found to be caused by a hitherto undescribed virus now named *Whassisvirus allo allo* which can be transmitted by the oral route (ie shouting) or in a suitable transport medium (eg police-horse manure). Virus gets into brain and causes unreasonable and provocative behaviour followed by overwhelming desire to run up and down pushing people. Many viruses are taken away for questioning and then deported to their country of origin which is found to be Italy.

Aerobics now shown to be a major cause of warts.

OCTOBER

Falling leaves shown to associated with minor degrees of concussion and is major cause of number of men wandering around public parks who can't remember what they're doing there when questioned.

Greece now shown to be a major cause of migraine.

Last year's report that people living under electricity pylons have a higher than normal incidence of suicide is re-examined. Earlier theories that the electricity in the cables exerted influence on human brains is shown to be totally false. Problem was that due to clerical errors people under pylons were being billed for electricity consumed by whole of Kent. People offered re-housing under North Sea Oil pipeline.

NOVEMBER

Major revelations in the self-medication market. Aspirin found to cause excessive ear-wax, Paracetamol found to cause athlete's foot and hot lemon juice found to cause premature ejaculation. Only good news is that the common cold is now shown not to be harmful in any way and may be good for you since clearing of secretions along mucosal pathways (ie down nostrils, over lip and on to shirt-front) may prepare body for new awareness of fresh experiences. Particularly another cold. Recent radiocative tracers in sinus sprays and similar aerosols show that particles of spray enter brain and clear inside of brain of any inflammation, memory and coherent thought. Excessive use, however, may thin the parietal cortex and if continued may seriously damage the ozone layer.

America is found to be a major cause of everything. World Health Organisation ask that United States be thoroughly disinfected. President Reagan asks where American people will live while this is being done. Puerto Rico says they can come back to their place.

DECEMBER

Most major 1985 health scares fizzle out. Jogger's baldness found to be curable by dunking head in mineral water (Malvern for straight hair, Perrier for curly); green monkey disease found to be psychological since monkey was jealous of his neighbour's nuts; Southern Comfort found to be less toxic than ginseng and huge reserves discovered under the North Sea; break dancing is found to cure herpes; a rare degenerative disease affecting paper is found to have caused the weakness of sterling and the new pound coin is innoculated against it.

Christmas Eve: Bishop of Durham hints at possibility that immaculate conception may have been caused by a virus.

COLOUR YOUR OWN OUT-PATIENTS DEPARTMENT

Just use our made-simple chart to transform your own clinic into a designer-made world of colour.

1 Mediterranean Beige
2 Early Morning Beige
3 Beige en Cocotte
4 Striped Beige
5 Yak
6 Biliary Beige
7 Beige Emmanuelle II
8 Enigma (Beige)
9 Ordinary Beige (Drab)
10 Beige Surprise
11 Dung Beige
12 Dungroamin'
13 Beige of the Train
14 Mistaken Beige
15 Angel Whip Beige
16 Beige Vindaloo
17 Papal Beige
18 Ecstasy (Beige)
19 Dial-a-Beige
20 Colloquial Beige
21 Bogie
22 Rush-hour Beige
23 Gravy
24 Brilliant White Beige
25 Knicker Beige
26 Boring (Beige)
27 Fantasy in Beige
28 Lapsang Souchong
29 Stagnant Beige
30 French Model (Beige)
31 Beige Bouillabaisse
32 Electric Blue (Beige)
33 Urinary Beige
34 Aboriginal Beige
35 Campbell's Condensed Beige
36 Beige No. 7
37 Hush Puppy
38 Pubic Beige
39 Beige Colour
40 Inter-Galactic Beige
41 Beige of Biscay
42 Nonstick Beige
43 Geoffrey Howe (Beige)
44 Pillarbox Beige
45 Clandestine (Beige)
46 Midnight Beige
47 Beige of Reason
48 Beige Mat
49 Eine Kleine Nachtbeige
50 Orgasm (Beige)
51 Beige à Hovis
52 Naval Beige
53 Beige Boy
54 Mouse Belly
55 Bilge Beige
56 Esprit (Beige)
57 Continuous Beige
58 Earwax
59 Herbeigeous Border
60 Beige Three
61 Tora Tora Tora
62 Intestinal Beige
63 Rainbow Beige
64 Moulting Retriever
65 Beige Already
66 Beige Ring of Confidence
67 Deep Fried Crispy Beige
68 Piles of Beige
69 Dandruff

Undercoat: Use 1603 (Beige) or 021 472 639 (Beige)